The Hearing-Impaired An Employee: Untapped Resource

The Hearing-Impaired Employee: An Untapped Resource

Coordinated by
Georgene Fritz and
Nancy Smith

 COLLEGE-HILL PRESS, San Diego, California

College-Hill Press
4284 41st Street
San Diego, California 92105

Library of Congress Cataloging in Publication Data

Fritz, Georgene.
    The hearing-impaired employee.

    Includes index.
    1. Hearing impaired—Employment—United States.
2. Personnel management—United States. I. Smith,
Nancy, 1950–   II. Title.
HV2551.F75   1984   658.3'045   84-22963
ISBN 0-88744-108-4

Printed in the United States of America

Foreword

As director of the National Technical Institute for the Deaf at Rochester Institute of Technology (NTID at RIT), I am pleased to offer *The Hearing-Impaired Employee: An Untapped Resource* to current and future employers of hearing-impaired people.

I would like to commend NTID's National Center on Employment of the Deaf (NCED), an international authority on advancing career opportunities for deaf people, for recognizing the need for this resource for both employers and employees.

Special appreciation also is extended to project coordinators Georgene Fritz and Nancy Smith for consolidating material from 19 content experts into this usable teaching manual.

Dr. William E. Castle

Vice President,
Rochester Institute of Technology

Director,
National Technical Institute for the Deaf

INTRODUCTION

Deafness — the inability to hear spoken language — is an invisible disability. There are no wheelchairs, leg braces, or red-tipped canes to indicate that a person is hearing impaired.

People who have had little experience with deafness tend to group hearing-impaired people into one category: "different" or "handicapped" or "not like us." But hearing-impaired people are individuals just like other people. They vary in their likes, dislikes, interests, and values. Even their hearing impairments can range from a slight hearing loss to complete inability to hear spoken language.

Whether a person has a hearing impairment or normal hearing, he/she is an individual and brings a unique set of skills, abilities, and career mobility expectations to a job. Helping a worker use his/her skills for the good of the organization is a major part of a supervisor's job.

This resource manual was developed to educate supervisors, trainers, and employers. It provides:

a general orientation to deafness and its impact on hearing-impaired employees

supervisory techniques for use with hearing-impaired employees

strategies for modifying training and the workplace to meet the needs of hearing-impaired employees

resources to use in making accommodations for hearing-impaired employees

This manual will help supervisors work more effectively with hearing-impaired employees. Some of these suggestions also may be useful when dealing with hearing people. Many of these tips simply are ways to help any employee become a more productive "member of the team."

Hiring a hearing-impaired employee not only affects the work of the supervisor, but also that of the employee's co-workers. For this reason, several sections of this manual can be used to orient all workers to the characteristics and needs of a hearing-impaired co-worker.

The following directory provides some commonly asked questions about deafness and deaf people, and shows you where to find the answers.

CONTENTS

DIRECTORY

Answers to Common Questions About the Employment
of Hearing-Impaired People

Is there something we can do to help hearing-impaired people adjust on-the-job? 50-53

Will we need to adapt our training program for these new employees? 56-63, 73, 88

We use a lot of audio materials and equipment in meetings and training — how can we use these with hearing-impaired people? 88-95

Is it unsafe for deaf people to work in industrial areas? 105-107

How will having this person around affect our other employees? 50, 70, 117-119

PART I:

HEARING IMPAIRMENT:

Its Potential Impact on the Individual

Some people might find Tim's speech difficult to understand. In turn, if Tim can't see your face, he might not understand your message, either.

Everyone is handicapped in one way or another. Most golfers have handicaps, but Bob Hope's hasn't prevented him from playing with presidents on national TV.

Similarly, Tim's handicap hasn't prevented him from competing successfully as an accountant at IBM, where he has earned recognition and promotion for his professional achievements.

FACTS AND COMMON MISCONCEPTIONS

WHAT IS A HEARING IMPAIRMENT?

A hearing impairment is a loss of hearing for some or all
parts (frequencies) of the sounds which occur around us.
Individual hearing losses are different. Just as people
have varying degrees of visual problems, hearing losses
also range from mild to profound. Such variations occur
because there are two parts to a hearing loss:

*loudness: Sounds need to
be louder than normal to
be heard. Some sounds,
however, may never be
loud enough to be
heard.*

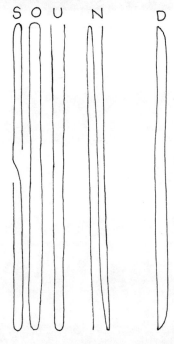

*clarity: Sounds that are
heard may be unclear or
cannot be understood at
all.*

Both of these parts vary in degree. A person whose primary hearing problem is loudness will have a different understanding of speech than someone for whom clarity is a problem. A person with a "loudness" problem usually will find it much easier to understand speech if the sounds can be made loud enough. This will not be true of a person with a clarity problem.

The real problem with a hearing impairment is not the loss of hearing, but the barrier to communication it creates. To better understand the impact that a hearing impairment has on a person's daily life, consider these scenarios which illustrate the average workday of two people, one hearing and one hearing impaired.

one hearing and ★ one hearing impaired.

In the home of the hearing employee, the alarm clock rings. This is the first of many sounds which alert family members that another workday has begun. Flick! On goes the light. A few seconds later, water pounds the walls of the shower stall. The coffee pot perks in the kitchen while a radio announcer reads the local news. The kitchen resounds with lively chatter as the family gathers around the breakfast table. Finally, the front door slams and the car engine roars to life.

★ In the home of the hearing-impaired employee, a different scene occurs. Flashing lights accompany the sound of the alarm clock, signaling it is time to wake up. Lights switch on and off to gain the attention of hearing-impaired family members.

★ Some hearing-impaired family members put on hearing aids. Hands and lips move, voices speak, and conversation starts. Breakfast is eaten, dishes are washed, and always the air is filled with some sounds, as well as the movement of hands or taps on the shoulder or arm. Soon the front door closes and the car starts.

When the hearing employee arrives on the job, he is greeted by welcoming voices. Throughout the day, conversations about a local clothing sale, politics, work, food prices, the weather, and bowling scores can be heard. At quitting time, calls of "Good night," "Take care," and "See you tomorrow" are heard.

★ For the hearing-impaired employee, the workday is different. When he walks through the door, he is met with mouths moving and some spoken sounds. Some words can be seen and understood. Such things as "Hi, how are you?" and "yesterday," "football," and "wonderful" are picked up easily. The employee sees smiling faces and receives pats on the arm or back. All around him he can see people talking. At one point, he notices a group laughing together. He wonders what they find so funny. At lunch, someone asks him what he thought of a television special which aired the night before. He says he did not watch the show—it was not captioned. (Captioned television programs translate spoken words or narration into printed words on the screen.)

Finally, it is quitting time. It has been a long day. The effort needed to do his work and to communicate with his co-workers has left him tired. Co-workers pat him on the back and say ''Good night.'' He thinks to himself, ''It will be nice to go home and communicate easily with someone.''

Being hearing impaired is much like being a visitor in a foreign country. You speak your language and the natives speak theirs. Although you can understand some of what each other says, it is frustrating because so much is missed. You cannot take part in group conversations and you usually miss out on jokes. Relaxing is difficult, since you must work so hard to understand what the natives are saying.

Being hearing impaired is also like visiting a foreign country in that the natives have habits and customs different from those in your homeland. Hearing people do not wave their hands, stomp on the floor, pound on desks, or touch another person's arm to gain attention. They also do not stand close together so they can see each other's lips clearly. Hearing people can listen to radios, understand uncaptioned television programs, and attend concerts — things not done by many hearing-impaired people.

For hearing-impaired people, traveling in a foreign land never really ends. When hearing-impaired people gather at home or for social events, they all can ''fit in'' because they can communicate easily and effectively with one another. But hearing-impaired people must spend time with hearing people. Rarely can they earn a living while associating only with other hearing-impaired people. Hearing-impaired people thus have to make a special effort to adjust to the work environment, an environment which is different from that of home. This adjustment is made much easier when co-workers are patient and supportive.

WHAT ARE THE DIFFERENCES BETWEEN "HEARING IMPAIRED," "DEAF," AND "HARD OF HEARING"?

A *hearing-impaired person* is one who has a hearing loss, and may be deaf or hard of hearing.

A *deaf person* is someone whose hearing loss is so severe that only very loud sounds, if any, are heard. Those sounds which are heard are not clear. This makes it difficult for the deaf person to hear and understand speech, even when it is louder. For all practical purposes, a deaf person usually cannot understand speech through hearing alone.

A *hard-of-hearing person* is someone whose hearing loss is not as severe as that of a deaf person. His/her ability to hear and understand speech (when it is made louder) is somewhat better than that of a deaf person.

WHAT CAUSES HEARING IMPAIRMENT?

There are many causes of hearing impairment, but some of the more common are:

heredity (passed on by parents, although they may not be hearing impaired)

accident (often a head injury)

birth injury

maternal rubella (mother had German measles during pregnancy)

aging

illness (diseases such as measles, mumps, and spinal meningitis)

Many cases of hearing impairment, however, are due to unknown causes.

WHY DO SOME HEARING-IMPAIRED PEOPLE SPEAK BETTER THAN OTHERS?

Oral language is learned by listening. Children learn to speak by listening to what others say and then mimicking them. Most children with normal hearing have learned to speak reasonably well by the time they are 3 to 6 years old.

If a hearing loss is present at birth or before the age of 3, it will be more difficult for the person to learn to speak, read, and write a language because he/she has never heard it spoken. If the loss occurs after age 3, the person will be able to speak, read, and write better. If the loss occurs after age 12 or 13, the person typically will have good reading, writing, and speaking skills, but difficulty understanding others.

The difference between a person born hearing impaired and one who becomes hearing impaired as an adult will be his/her knowledge of spoken language. Persons who become hearing impaired as adults will be able to speak well, with few flaws in their speech. However, these persons may not necessarily be exceptional in their speechreading abilities.

The quality of the speech of a person born hearing impaired or who became hearing impaired at an early age depends upon things such as:

the age at which the loss was discovered and when the use of hearing aids began

how much hearing remains

how motivated the person was to learn to speak

the type of training provided and at what age it began

HOW MIGHT THE SPEECH OF A HEARING-IMPAIRED PERSON BE DIFFERENT FROM THAT OF A HEARING PERSON?

A hearing-impaired person's speech may sound very much like that of a person with normal hearing. When differences do occur, it is because it is hard for hearing-impaired persons to make sounds which they cannot hear themselves or others saying.

In some cases, the speech differences may be as slight as a lisp. For others, you may hear such things as:

1. sounds produced alike (because they are heard that way) which should not be alike (such as ''fin,'' ''sin,'' and ''thin'' all sounding like ''fin'')

2. sounds which are not heard (by that person) are left out

3. little words (on, in, a), parts of words (-s, -ed, -ing), and some sounds (k, g, h) that are hard to hear or see on the lips may be left out

4. words used in the wrong order

5. words mispronounced

6. abnormal pitch and rhythm

The more you hear the speech of a hearing-impaired individual, the more understandable it will become for you.

DO HEARING AIDS HELP?

Hearing aids are helpful for many hearing-impaired people. But they are not a solution to deafness because they only can deal with one part of a hearing loss: loudness. They do little to make unclear sounds clearer, and they cannot make it possible to hear frequencies for which no hearing remains.

To understand this better, think about tuning in a radio station. You faintly hear a favorite song being played. When you turn up the volume, you can hear the song pretty well.

For some hearing-impaired people, using a hearing aid is just like turning up the volume on a car radio. For others, however, a hearing aid is not as helpful.

If the radio station you are listening to has a weak signal, even with a higher volume, there is static. The sound is unclear and fades in and out. From moment to moment, sounds change from loud-and-clear, to loud-and-unclear, to not-loud-enough, to no sound at all. Even with a hearing aid, some hearing-impaired people may hear things this way.

For those with no hearing left, hearing aids may be useless. Fortunately, such cases are rare.

WHAT ABOUT THE TELEPHONE — CAN HEARING-IMPAIRED PEOPLE USE IT?

Some hearing-impaired people can use the telephone; others cannot. This depends on several factors. The hearing-impaired person with whom you work can tell you about his/her ability to use the telephone. However, any hearing-impaired person who can read and write can learn to use a TDD (Telecommunication Device for the Deaf) to send and receive messages transmitted over telephone lines.

CAN HEARING-IMPAIRED PEOPLE TOLERATE NOISY WORK AREAS BETTER THAN HEARING PEOPLE?

No. Like a hearing person, the hearing-impaired worker should use ear protection in areas with high noise levels. It is rare for a hearing-impaired person to have no hearing at all. Depending upon the type of loss, a hearing-impaired person may find it uncomfortable to work in noisy areas. Worse, dangerously high noise levels can damage the person's residual (remaining) hearing.

I DON'T KNOW SIGN LANGUAGE. WILL I BE ABLE TO COMMUNICATE WITH HEARING-IMPAIRED PEOPLE?

Not all hearing-impaired people have the same communication skills. Many hearing-impaired people use sign language, but certainly not all of them. Any time communication is attempted, there are at least two people involved: the person sending the message (the speaker) and the person receiving it (the listener). The way in which the message is sent must match the needs and skills of the person receiving it.

Depending on your skills and those of the hearing-impaired person with whom you are trying to communicate, the two of you can use speech, listening, speechreading, sign language, facial expressions, gestures, mime (acting out the idea), writing, drawing pictures, or a combination of any or all of these. As a hearing person, you already know how to use most of these methods. Only speechreading and sign language are likely to be new for you.

A REMINDER:
If you are uncertain
which methods a
hearing-impaired
person prefers, ask.

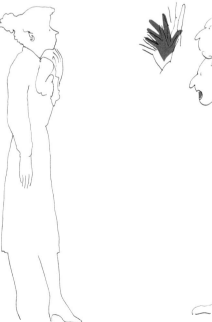

METHODS OF COMMUNICATION

People with normal hearing usually communicate by talking and listening. Often, they pay attention only to the words that are spoken and the tone of voice used to say them. Moreover, most people also use facial expressions and gestures to emphasize their words. Faces, hands, and arms can be very useful tools when communicating with others.

In the illustration, the speaker is saying "I don't know." Notice how the message is much clearer when the speaker below uses his face and body to emphasize his words.

Facial expressions and body movements are especially important when talking with a hearing-impaired person.

Hearing-impaired people may, with hearing aids, hear some of what is said, but it may not sound much like what people with normal hearing would hear. Because of this, it is important to make spoken messages as visible as possible. Usually a combination of methods works well.

Remember that hearing-impaired people vary widely in
the ways in which they communicate, and the skill with
which they do it. However, most hearing-impaired
people communicate using:

listening   speechreading

facial expressions and
gestures

mime (acting out   drawings   writing
the idea)

sign language

                                                a combination of any
                        speech   or all of these

Since you already know how to do most of these, let's
look at two you may not know much about:

speechreading   **sign language**

WHAT IS SPEECHREADING?

Speechreading involves watching a person's mouth and face to read what words are being said. Since hearing-impaired people usually cannot hear speech as it normally sounds, they may use their eyes to try to make up for what they cannot hear.

It is important to understand that:

Not all hearing-impaired people read speech as easily and accurately as hearing people can listen to it.

Not all hearing-impaired people who became deaf as adults can automatically speechread. For them, like others, it is a skill which must be learned and practiced regularly.

Not all hearing-impaired people are skilled at speechreading.

Research studies have found that only about three out of every 10 words can be speechread clearly. Speechreading is a little bit like trying to take a fill-in-the-blank test such as this:

"We __ __ __ you
__ __ __ __
today."

The complete sentence is:
We all appreciate what you have done for us today.

That isn't easy to figure out, is it? Speechreading is difficult since only 30-40 percent of speech is visible. Many words that are visible have the same mouth movement (and look the same on the lips), but sound different.

For example, see how "pan" and "ban" look the same on the lips. The same is true of "fan" and "fin." There are many more words like these that can easily be confused by speechreaders. Because of this, speechreaders often must guess what was said.

Some hearing-impaired people are good speechreaders; others are not. Speechreading, like any new skill, is more likely to be acquired if the person:

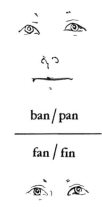

ban / pan

fan / fin

receives the training needed	practices the skill regularly
receives encouragement from others	has some natural ability in that area
	has some previously developed skill in that area

Learning to speechread also is easier if the person's hearing loss occurred after language was learned.

Some hearing-impaired people are more successful at speechreading than others because they can hear some of what is said. People who can both watch lip movements and hear some sounds have an advantage over those who can only watch lips move.

To understand how difficult speechreading is, try turning off the sound while watching the evening news on television. Then watch the announcer's lips and facial expressions. If you are like most people, you will find it difficult to follow much of the broadcast. Now think about the advantages you would have trying to speechread in such a situation.

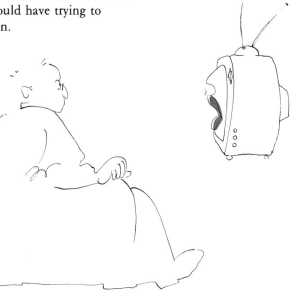

Although you lack training in this skill, you have:

a speaker who does not turn away or move around while talking

some pictures to indicate the subject being discussed

lips to watch that are not covered by a mustache, beard, cigarette, pencil, or drinking cup

the well-lighted face of a speaker you have seen and heard before

the ability to read, write, and speak the language

one person talking at a time

In addition, you may have heard some of the information that was reported earlier in the day.

Believe it or not, other than your lack of training, the conditions under which you would be speechreading are outstanding!

Since speechreading is a complex skill which people may or may not acquire easily, even with years of practice, a supervisor should not expect a hearing-impaired employee to greatly improve his/her skills if requested. Instead, a speechreader should be encouraged to use his/her skills and hearing people should try to make conditions conducive to speechreading.

Fortunately, the hearing-impaired person may be better able to speechread what you say once he/she becomes used to:

the way you speak

the topics the two of you usually discuss

the words you usually use

Some hearing-impaired people can understand everyday conversations by speechreading; others need sign language to understand what is being communicated.

WHAT IS SIGN LANGUAGE?

Sign language is a way of communicating words, ideas, and feelings using the body (mainly hands, arms, and face). There are two main parts to sign language:

fingerspelling   and   signs

Fingerspelling involves using handshapes to represent letters of the alphabet. There is a different handshape for each letter. Letters can be formed one after another to spell out words. When "written in the air," the word *friend* looks like this:

Signs are like words because each one has a meaning associated with it. A sign is made up of a unique set of movements, handshapes, and hand positions. The sign for *friend* looks like this:

Ideas can be expressed more easily and dramatically with signs than with fingerspelling. However, fingerspelling is very useful when:

there isn't a sign for a word (or you don't know one)

the person receiving the message doesn't know the sign for a word

it is important for the other person to know the exact spelling of the word

Together, signs and fingerspelling help make communication faster and more accurate for many hearing-impaired people.

DO HEARING-IMPAIRED PEOPLE ALL OVER THE COUNTRY USE THE SAME SIGNS?

Some signs vary within different parts of the United States, much the way hearing people say "pancakes," "griddlecakes," "flapjacks," or "flannelcakes," depending on where they live. There also is more than one sign language system.

Some people use what is called Ameslan or ASL (American Sign Language). Other people sign in English. The most common form of signing English is Pidgin Sign English (PSE).

WHAT IS THE DIFFERENCE BETWEEN ASL AND PSE?

<u>ASL</u> is a language, separate from English, that is used by many hearing-impaired people in the United States and Canada. For example, in English, the question: *What cities have you been to?* would be signed in ASL: "cities you (touch finish)?"

The signs for "touch" and "finish" here mean "been to" or "experienced."

Hearing-impaired children usually learn ASL from their deaf parents or friends. It usually is not used in the classroom, although this is now changing. There is no spoken form of ASL and there currently is no standardized way of writing it.

<u>PSE</u> involves the use of ASL signs in English word order. Sometimes fingerspelling and newly developed signs are used to represent English grammar. Although two or more spoken words may be represented with one sign, PSE can closely match signs with the words used in an English sentence.

<u>PSE</u> is the most common sign language system used by hearing people. It is the system most often used by teachers of hearing-impaired people. Hearing-impaired people often will sign in ASL to one another and sign in PSE with hearing people.

Regardless of the sign language system used, a signer can show different meanings with the same signs. Hearing people do this by changing their tone of voice. Signers do this with:

body language

how large or small the sign is made

the direction in which the sign is made

eye movements

facial expressions

It is important to realize, however, that not all hearing-impaired people have the same sign language skills. Some may know ASL, fingerspelling, and signed English, while others may know only one or none of these.

WHY DO SOME HEARING-IMPAIRED PEOPLE SIGN USING THEIR VOICE, WHILE OTHERS DO NOT?

Some hearing-impaired people use "simultaneous communication." This means that the person talks and signs at the same time. Others may sign and not use their voice. There are three common reasons why a hearing-impaired person would not use his/her voice while signing:

ASL is being used and this language does not use the voice

he/she is communicating with a hearing-impaired person who does not speechread and/or have any residual hearing

the person is not comfortable using his/her voice

SHOULD I LEARN SIGN LANGUAGE?

First, you should determine what method of communication is preferred by the hearing-impaired person with whom you work. If he/she uses sign language, you may want to take a course in sign language.

WHERE ARE SIGN LANGUAGE COURSES TAUGHT?

In most cities, community colleges and continuing education programs offer sign language courses. You may find out about courses by contacting:

clubs for the deaf

special education departments in nearby colleges and universities

local chapters of the National Association of the Deaf (NAD)

associations for hearing-impaired people

The hearing-impaired person with whom you work also may know where you can take a sign language course or may be willing to teach you and others.

SIGN LANGUAGE SEEMS REALLY COMPLICATED. WILL IT BE HARD FOR ME TO LEARN?

Whether or not sign language is difficult to learn depends on the individual. Some find it easy and fun, while others find it more difficult. The best way to learn is by:

communicating with skilled signers

practicing and using your signing skills daily

taking a course

Remember, you do not have to become a highly skilled signer. In fact, you can communicate with a hearing-impaired person by using speech, natural gestures, body language, and writing — all with or without using sign language.

WHAT DO INTERPRETERS DO?

Interpreters facilitate communication between hearing and hearing-impaired people. Interpreters can sign (with or without mouthing) what a hearing person says for hearing-impaired people who use sign language. Interpreters can voice what a hearing-impaired person signs for those hearing people who do not know sign language. Interpreters also can mouth what a hearing person says for hearing-impaired people who speechread. This latter method helps the hearing-impaired person understand the message, regardless of whether the speaker's face is visible.

IS IT ALL RIGHT TO USE WRITING AS A WAY OF COMMUNICATING WITH A HEARING-IMPAIRED PERSON?

Yes, it is an acceptable way of communicating. This method can be a bit slow, particularly for those of us accustomed to rapid verbal exchanges. However, this slower pace may make it possible to identify points of misunderstanding quickly. Short notes are the easiest for everyone — including hearing-impaired people — to read and write. Aside from the time required, written communication may reveal weaknesses in the writing skills of some hearing-impaired people. Nevertheless, do not hesitate to use this mode of communication, especially when other methods have not been found satisfactory.

ARE THERE ANY RULES TO FOLLOW WHEN TALKING TO A HEARING-IMPAIRED PERSON?

There are no absolute rules to follow. Remember, however, that hearing-impaired people prefer to communicate directly with the person to whom they are talking. Keep in mind that when both people involved really *want* to communicate with each other, they usually find a way to succeed.

Using these concepts, there are some things you *can* do to make communication easier for you and your hearing-impaired employee.

When You First Meet a Hearing-Impaired Person

Observe how the hearing-impaired person usually communicates with hearing people

Ask the hearing-impaired person what you can do to make it easier for the two of you to communicate

Check to make sure the hearing-impaired person really understands you by re-phrasing your questions or demonstrating what you mean

Each Time You Start a Conversation

Get the hearing-impaired person's attention by using a tap on the shoulder, a wave of the hand, or some other visible signal

Move away from background noise so that the hearing-impaired person's hearing aid can be helpful

Stand or sit in a well lighted area. Neither of you should be in front of a strong light (it makes shadows on your faces) or in a dimly lighted area

Give (or ask for) a hint of what topic is going to be discussed. This can be done either by pointing to something or writing out a sentence or two

Take time to communicate. Try not to appear rushed, impatient, or disinterested. That will discourage the hearing-impaired person from trying to communicate with you

When You Are the Speaker

Do not speak louder than usual. Shouting is impolite, confusing if the hearing-impaired person is wearing a hearing aid, and probably useless if an aid is not used

Speak slowly and clearly, but do not exaggerate mouth movements

Use natural gestures and facial expressions. It always is easier to understand a lively speaker

Look directly at the hearing-impaired person, even if an interpreter is being used. If you turn your face, the hearing-impaired person may have difficulty seeing your lips and/or facial expressions

Avoid smoking, eating, drinking, or putting your hands in front of your mouth while you are speaking

Stay in one place while speaking. Watching the lips of a pacing speaker is difficult

Use short sentences and repeat them if they are not understood the first time

If something is not understood after it has been repeated once, re-phrase the message using simpler words or the same words in a different order. Sometimes the lack of understanding is due to a group of lip movements which are hard to speechread

If you must use words that you think the hearing-impaired person may not know, write them down. Then explain them. It is unlikely that someone can speechread an unfamiliar word

Ask questions to make sure your message was understood

If you have a beard or mustache, keep the hair around the mouth trimmed. Lip movements hidden by hair are hard to detect

Keep in mind that only three out of every 10 spoken words are visible; therefore, even a skilled speechreader will have to make some guesses about what was said

When You Are the Listener

Encourage the hearing-impaired person to speak, but do not force the issue if he/she does not want to speak

Listen carefully to what the speaker says

Pay attention to the speaker's facial expressions and gestures

Ask for the message to be repeated if you do not understand it. If you pretend to understand when you don't, you will have problems later

Ask questions to make sure you really did understand the message

AND REMEMBER!

Do not hesitate to use paper and pencil to make sure there is communication. Written notes are far better than misunderstanding.

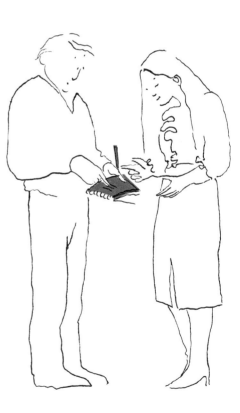

READING AND WRITING SKILLS

Hearing-impaired people, like hearing people, vary widely in how well they can read and write. However, there are some general things that can be said about the reading and writing skills of hearing-impaired people.

As a group, hearing-impaired people do not read or write as well as hearing people with the same amount of education. Fifty percent of hearing high school graduates read at or above the 12th grade level, whereas only 10 percent of hearing-impaired high school graduates will be able to read at or above the 8th grade level. These are the students most likely to go on to college. The average hearing-impaired person who completes high school will read at about the 4th grade level.

This difference in reading skills is not because hearing-impaired people do not have the same potential as hearing people; it is because they often do not have the same opportunities as hearing people to learn the language.

Hearing people learn to speak by listening to others talk and repeating what they say. By the time most hearing people are 3-6 years old, they can speak fairly well. When they enter school, they learn to read and write the words they already know how to say. As they grow older, they learn how to say, read, and write more and more words — words which have been heard.

Acquisition of language is a developmental process. It doesn't happen overnight, regardless of how capable or motivated the learner is. For people born hearing impaired, or those who become hearing impaired before the age of 3, this developmental process is impeded. Unlike hearing people, hearing-impaired people cannot learn language only by listening. Instead, language is learned by watching the "silent movies" of life around them. Parents and teachers of hearing-impaired children must work hard to help them learn what hearing children learn by listening. Hearing people can continue to hear (and learn) new words, but the hearing-impaired person, despite extra efforts, may not be able to learn the language as well as someone who hears normally.

One who becomes hearing impaired while school-aged or as an adult usually will not have as much difficulty reading and writing as someone who was born hearing impaired or who lost his/her hearing at an early age, assuming that the person could read and write before the hearing loss occurred.

**Matching Reading Skills
and Assigned Tasks**

First, identify what type of reading must be done. There is a whole range of reading materials, each requiring the reader to use different reading skills.

The following chart shows a scale of reading materials ranging from the easiest to read and understand to the most difficult.

new information not
directly related to
one's field of work
(most difficult)

main points and
supporting details in
readings about one's
field of work

main points in
readings about one's
field of work

brief directions about
an unfamiliar task

brief directions about
a familiar task

short notes
(easiest)

Many hearing-impaired people will be successful reading short notes or directions. Some will have difficulty with other kinds of reading. If a person seems unable to read and answer questions about written materials, you can either:

| rewrite some of the materials | or | have someone who understands the materials (and can communicate with the hearing-impaired person) explain those parts which are not understood |

People who have difficulty reading invariably will also have weaknesses in their written work. People who read well can use examples of correctly written material as models for their own writing. Poor readers, however, cannot do this. This is because poor readers will be unable to recognize the difference between well written and poorly written materials, since they have difficulty reading both types.

Assessing Writing Skills

As with reading skills, the writing skills of hearing-impaired people vary widely. Writing tasks, like reading tasks, can range from the easiest to write to the most difficult. This scale shows the range:

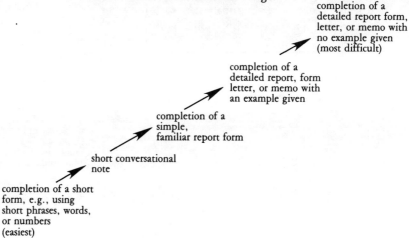

completion of a detailed report form, letter, or memo with no example given (most difficult)

completion of a detailed report, form letter, or memo with an example given

completion of a simple, familiar report form

short conversational note

completion of a short form, e.g., using short phrases, words, or numbers (easiest)

Although many hearing-impaired employees will have a good command of English writing skills, particularly if they possess advanced educational degrees, errors in writing usually will fall into one of five categories:

1. There are no mistakes in grammar or in the words used, but some spelling and punctuation errors can be found. The writing of many hearing people falls into this group.

2. Some word ending errors (such as 'ed' instead of 'ing') are present. This type of writing is easy to understand and errors can be corrected by a secretary.

3. Whole words are used incorrectly, such as nouns — people, places, or things — used instead of action words.

4. Major parts of sentences are left out or placed in the wrong order.

5. Ideas are not organized clearly or facts are stated incorrectly.

It is possible to match the hearing-impaired person's assigned tasks with his/her writing skills by reviewing a sample of the person's writing. Polished reading and writing skills are the result of years of training, practice, and patience. Since such skills are acquired slowly, deficiencies (particularly with adults) cannot be remedied quickly. Efforts to do so may yield limited results, especially when the weaknesses are severe. Although it may be beneficial for a hearing-impaired employee to be encouraged to receive additional training in English skills, a supervisor should be realistic about the amount of improvement which can be demonstrated in long-standing problem areas.

The types of errors found in the writing that fits into categories 3 and 4 cause major problems for the reader unless he/she is very familiar with the topic.

Category 5 errors usually are caused by the writer not understanding the topic he/she was asked to write about, in addition to weaknesses in his/her writing skills.

If an employee (hearing or hearing impaired) has writing skills like those in categories 3, 4, or 5, writing tasks should not be a major part of his/her job unless they are improved. Additional training may or may not enable employees displaying these skills to improve them to the level shown in categories 1 and 2. Employees whose writing is like that in categories 1 and 2 may show benefit from additional training. Such people can easily be productive in jobs requiring written work.

PART II:

HEARING-IMPAIRED JOB CANDI

TES: Recruiting Them

Tim had a chance to work for
IBM as a co-op student during
his junior year at college. That
was all he needed — a chance.
Tim did so well that IBM
offered him a job before he
started his senior year.

*When Tim graduated, he
didn't have to look for a job:
IBM was looking for him.*

*Tim may be hearing impaired,
but when opportunity knocked,
he listened.*

WAYS OF LOCATING QUALIFIED APPLICANTS

The phrase 'progressive employment' means actively recruiting and hiring competent disabled persons for positions in a company. By seeking out, interviewing and hiring qualified candidates, regardless of their physical disabilities, a company can be assured of hiring the best possible people.

Gone are the days when hearing-impaired people were confined to a few occupations. Hearing-impaired people today are employed in fields ranging from electromechanical engineering to medical technology and architectural drafting. In 1983, there were more than 100 postsecondary education programs for hearing-impaired people in the United States. This means increased educational opportunities for all hearing-impaired people. Because of the availability of support services (tutors, notetakers, and interpreters) at these and other postsecondary institutions, hearing-impaired people now can receive training in career areas previously closed to them. The majority of these are technical or professional areas.

With increased training opportunities, hearing-impaired people are as qualified and competent as their hearing counterparts. And like hearing people, hearing-impaired people seek jobs which are challenging and provide opportunities for career advancement. Unfortunately, these opportunities are fewer than for hearing people because many employers continue to believe outdated stereotypes of disabled people. They may think that hearing-impaired workers cannot perform jobs as well as hearing workers. It is also common for employers and co-workers to think that all hearing-impaired people cannot speak, write intelligibly, or comprehend technical materials. Too often, they focus on what hearing-impaired people *cannot* do, rather than on what they *can* do. In order for a company to successfully adopt and implement progressive employment policy toward hearing-impaired people, all employees should be

For more information, see Appendix A.

briefed on hearing disabilities and the advantages of a progressive employment policy. Once employees at all levels become committed to the effort of hiring hearing-impaired people, everyone involved can look positively upon the presence of such workers within the company. Winning commitment from upper level management can often facilitate the successful placement of a hearing-impaired worker. In many organizations, gaining the support of this group, prior to introducing the idea to other groups within the organization, can spell the difference between success and failure.

Once commitment to the hiring of a hearing-impaired person has been developed within the company, qualified candidates for the position must be found.

The National Technical Institute for the Deaf (NTID) at Rochester Institute of Technology (RIT), is one source of information for locating qualified hearing-impaired applicants for a variety of technical positions. Contact the National Center on Employment of the Deaf, NTID at RIT, One Lomb Memorial Drive, Post Office Box 9887, Rochester, NY 14623. If you are seeking applicants in your immediate area, contact the local Office of Vocational Rehabilitation, the local branch of the National Association of the Deaf, the local club for the deaf, and/or regional educational programs for hearing-impaired people.

INTERVIEWING STRATEGIES

The objectives for interviewing hearing-impaired persons are no different than for hearing individuals. As an interviewer, you still want to learn about the candidate's

skills and abilities

motivation

work experience

educational history

interest in your company and the position

You seek qualified and competent candidates, regardless of whether they are hearing impaired or not. You want people who can do the job. However, with some basic information about hearing-impaired people, you can conduct interviews more efficiently.

Not all hearing-impaired people communicate in the same way. The *key* is finding a communication method that works best for you and the interviewee.

Depending on the interviewee's communication style, you may want to use an interpreter. Discuss this with the candidate prior to the interview. If an interpreter is used, you should talk directly to the candidate, *not* to the interpreter, and utilize the following techniques.

Interviewing Tips

To communicate with a hearing-impaired person in a one-to-one situation:

Get the hearing-impaired person's attention before speaking. A tap on the shoulder, a wave, or another visual signal usually does the trick.

Key the hearing-impaired person into the topic of discussion. Hearing-impaired people need to know what subject matter is to be discussed in order to pick up words which help them follow the conversation. This is especially important for hearing-impaired people who depend on oral communication.

Look directly at the hearing-impaired person when speaking. Even a slight turn of your head can obscure their speech-reading view.

Speak slowly and clearly, but do not yell, exaggerate or overpronounce. Exaggeration and overemphasis of words distorts lip movements, making speechreading more difficult. Try to enunciate each word without force or tension. Short sentences are easier to understand than long ones.

First repeat, then try to rephrase a thought rather than again repeating the same words. If the person only missed one or two words the first time, one repetition usually will help. Particular combinations of lip movements sometimes are difficult for hearing-impaired persons to speechread. Don't hesitate to write your message if necessary. Speechreading some words may be difficult. Getting the message across is more important than the medium used.

Do not place anything in your mouth when speaking. Mustaches that obscure the lips, smoking, pencil chewing, and putting your hands in front of your face all make it difficult for hearing-impaired persons to follow what is being said.

Maintain eye contact with the hearing-impaired person. Eye contact conveys the feeling of direct communication. Even if an interpreter is present, continue to speak directly to the hearing-impaired person. He/she will turn to the interpreter as needed.

Avoid standing in front of a light source, such as a window or bright light. The bright background and shadows created on the face make it almost impossible to speechread.

Use pantomime, body language, and facial expression to help communicate. A lively speaker always is more interesting to watch.

Be courteous to the deaf person during conversation. If the telephone rings or someone knocks at the door, excuse yourself and tell the hearing-impaired person that you are answering the phone or responding to the knock. Do not ignore the hearing-impaired person and carry on a conversation with someone else while the hearing-impaired person waits.

Use open-ended questions which must be answered by more than "yes" or "no." Do not assume that hearing-impaired persons have understood your message if they nod their head in acknowledgment. Open-ended questions ensure that your information has been communicated.

Some Additional Tips for Interviewing

These tips can be used in conjunction with the "one-to-one" tips to facilitate an interview with a hearing-impaired job applicant. They will make the interview more productive and comfortable for both the interviewer and the interviewee.

Provide company literature for the applicant to review *before* the interview. This helps the applicant become familiar with the company, its organization, products, and benefit programs.

Provide a written itinerary if the applicant is to be interviewed by more than one person. Include the names, titles, and meeting times for each individual the applicant will see. It often is difficult to speechread an unfamiliar person's title and name during a meeting. An itinerary allows the hearing-impaired person to be better informed, at ease, and able to follow up later if needed.

Inform your receptionist or secretary beforehand that you are expecting a hearing-impaired applicant for an interview. This will make it easier for the receptionist to assist the hearing-impaired person and facilitate any necessary paperwork.

GUIDELINES FOR TESTING

Hearing impairment is a communication barrier. It restricts or limits the hearing-impaired individual in his/her acquisition of information, and in many instances in the use of language.

Due to the potential language difficulties of hearing-impaired persons, the use of language tests to measure ability may not accurately reflect the hearing-impaired person's capabilities. If possible, use some other means of evaluation. If a test must be administered, use the following guidelines:

**Guidelines for
Test Givers**

Make sure the hearing-impaired candidate understands the directions and/or the purpose of the test.

Be sure the hearing-impaired candidate understands and/or can read the test material. The lack of ability to read test material may reflect a weakness in language rather than lack of technical knowledge. If possible, determine, through verbal questioning and/or demonstration or other means, if the technical knowledge is present before making a judgment on the individual's abilities. To determine whether a hearing-impaired person is able to read the material, have the person explain the meaning of 10 of the more important words/concepts to be read and understood (e.g., "clarify," "explain," "technical vocabulary"). If the person explains five of these words correctly, one can assume that he/she can read and comprehend the test material.

If possible, allow the individual to take extra time to comprehend the written message fully and complete the test. Many hearing-impaired persons do not perform well under timed test conditions which require reading and writing. This is because of the extra effort and time required to understand the written message in order to complete the required test.

PART III:

ON THE JOB:

Integrating The Hearing-Impaired Employee

*"Supervising Tim isn't without
its problems. He's young. He's
ambitious. He's still learning.
He makes mistakes. And
sometimes there are
communication problems."*

"More than anything else, it's rewarding to manage Tim. My job is to manage people and to see that they do their jobs well. Tim has added a new dimension to my job. It's helped keep my work and my life in perspective."

SOCIAL ADJUSTMENT

Everyone has experienced the awkwardness, anxiety, and excitement that come with a new job. The first few weeks always are a period of adjustment. The new employee must:

find out about the formal and informal systems by which the organization is run

develop social and working relationships with supervisors and co-workers

learn how to find his/her way around the work area

However, the new employee is not the only one who must adapt. Supervisors and co-workers also must make adjustments. They must learn how to interact effectively with the new employee. The length and difficulty of the adjustment period depends upon those involved.

Although all new employees require some "settling-in" time, the period may be longer and more anxiety-producing for a hearing-impaired employee because:

it is difficult for a hearing-impaired person to obtain spoken information especially in an unfamiliar setting

few hearing people have experience working and communicating with hearing-impaired people

A hearing-impaired person sometimes must work a bit harder to get the information needed to succeed on the job. While the hearing-impaired employee must determine how to communicate with a group of new people, supervisors and co-workers also must take time to acquire or improve the skills they need to interact well with their new co-worker.

There are ways the supervisor of the hearing-impaired employee can help all the employees through the adjustment period. Such assistance will produce cost-effective results for the company, which can be viewed in three ways:

the employee will be more likely to experience job satisfaction, resulting in a longer period of service with the company

a shorter period of time will be required before the new employee becomes a productive team member

the employee will continue to be productive because he/she knows what is expected on the job

How to Assist in Job Adjustment

Four ways to help hearing-impaired employees and their co-workers through the adjustment period are:

"buddy" or "mentoring" system

periodic meetings

inclusion in social gatherings

counseling sessions, if needed

name tags and introductions during the first few days

Name Tags and Introductions

A good way for a hearing-impaired person to become acquainted with other employees is to have everyone wear name tags during the new employee's first week. If this is not possible, co-workers should introduce themselves, write down their names, and talk a bit with the hearing-impaired employee.

Inclusion in Social Gatherings

When employees get together for a cup of coffee or lunch, someone should invite the hearing-impaired employee to join the group. Including the new employee in social gatherings helps break down the feelings of isolation. It may take a little time for everyone in the group to communicate easily with one another, but the more time spent together socially, the easier communication becomes.

*The Buddy or Mentoring
System*
With any new job, an employee may feel anxious and
uncertain. These feelings may be even more intense for
a hearing-impaired person because of the lack of
auditory information, communication difficulties, stress
resulting from trying to communicate, and/or lack of a
peer support group at the workplace. To help the newly
hired hearing-impaired employee better understand
his/her environment, it may be beneficial to assign a
"buddy" or "mentor" to this new person. This mentor
would be responsible for helping the new employee
understand information concerning:

insurance

employee benefits

company policy

general company
information

This person could also help clarify for the employee the
appropriate methods of interacting with various staff
members and any informal rules that exist, and answer
any work-related questions.

Periodic Meetings
All employees need feedback about their job
performance. Supervisors also need feedback about how
employees think and feel about their environment, their
jobs, and the people with whom they work. Supervisors
cannot deal effectively with problems in the workplace
without such information.

Because of potential communication complications, some
supervisors may slip into a pattern of avoiding serious
discussions with hearing-impaired employees. It is
important to schedule regular times for such discussions.
In this way, supervisors will get to know their employees
better and be able to head off potential problems. Such
discussions indicate to *all* employees that their
supervisors are concerned about the well-being of the
people with whom they work.

Counseling Services

Counseling offered by a qualified person can provide new employees with a safe way of communicating their perceptions about work, themselves, and their emotions. Some organizations may employ a staff psychologist or counselor. If so, this person also might be able to provide small group counseling for the supervisor and co-workers of a new employee, as well as individual sessions with the new employee. Of course, such services should be offered only if deemed appropriate for the individuals involved. If used, counseling services for a hearing-impaired employee should be offered by someone skilled in communicating with hearing-impaired people. If a trained professional is not available within your company, a personnel officer can determine what counseling services are available for hearing-impaired people within the community.

TECHNIQUES FOR SUPERVISORS

Hearing-impaired employees, like other employees, need supervision. Sometimes, people are reluctant to tell physically impaired employees exactly what to do, how to do it, and whether or not the results are satisfactory. However, the only way an employee can become an asset to an organization is by receiving feedback about job performance. The hearing-impaired employee needs access to, not protection from, the realities of the workplace.

Here are some practical steps you can take to become a successful supervisor of a hearing-impaired employee.

State exactly what the specific task will involve (in writing, when possible):

what is to be done

what level of accuracy is expected

when it is to be completed

when certain parts of the task are to be finished

at which points progress is to be checked with the supervisor

who can give help or advice

If appropriate, demonstrate the task to be done. It is much easier for people to understand what is to be done when they have seen the job performed.

When you have finished giving directions, make sure that the hearing-impaired person understood them. The best way to do this is to ask for an explanation or demonstration of what is to be done. Do not rely on a "yes" or "no" answer.

Be available to offer guidance when a project begins. This is when the employee is most likely to be uncertain about how he/she is to proceed.

Once a progress checkpoint has been reached, give the employee feedback on his/her performance. *Do not* wait until the entire project is completed. It then will be too late to correct any mistakes that occurred early in the process.

Motivate your employees by encouraging their efforts.

Only criticize those parts of the job which are done incorrectly. If you give negative feedback about an entire job when only parts of it are wrong, the employee may assume that the entire effort is worthless. He/she will not be certain how to go about doing the job right in the future.

Tell the person how pleased you are when a job has been done well. If you are silent, he/she may think you either are dissatisfied or disinterested.

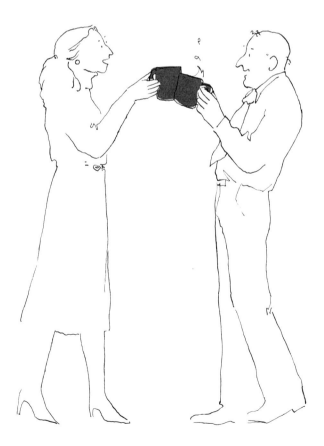

TRAINING PROCEDURES

Providing good training for employees is a challenge. Each employee brings a unique set of skills, interests, attitudes, and experience. When one or more trainees is hearing impaired, additional factors should be considered when planning and conducting training session(s). It will be necessary to determine the reading, writing, and communication skills of a hearing-impaired trainee.

Here are some factors to be considered when integrating hearing-impaired people into training programs:

organizing the presentation

determining appropriate teaching methods

arranging the classroom seating (learning environment)

simplifying written materials

setting the trainees' expectations

evaluating trainee progress

managing communication in the classroom

In this section, you will be given tips on how, within each of these areas, you can provide training which will meet the needs of all trainees, both hearing and hearing impaired. At the end of this section, you will find some *Helpful Hints* for working with hearing-impaired trainees.

Organizing the presentation

Information presented in a training session should follow a logical sequence. Because hearing-impaired people cannot receive spoken information as easily as hearing people, they will not learn as well if they have to figure out the relationships between bits and pieces of information. These relationships can be made clear by:

presenting related pieces of information one after the other

stating how the pieces are related to one another (for example, first, second, third, etc. or small parts of a larger system)

showing the relationship in some concrete way (using items such as pictures or actual objects)

The best course to follow is to:

introduce the idea or piece of information

present examples of that idea or information

present related ideas or information

provide more examples

Before moving on to a new subject unrelated to what has been presented before, be sure to let the hearing-impaired trainee know that this is going to occur.

Determining appropriate teaching methods

Most trainees like variety in the training session. They may be ready for a change even before the trainer is aware that they have become tired or bored with the current activity.

The hearing-impaired trainee has the added problem of visual fatigue. Since hearing-impaired people must constantly use their eyes to receive information, they need frequent breaks to relax their eyes. If an interpreter is used, he/she also will need breaks. The way to keep all trainees attentive is to vary the way in which information is presented throughout the training session. Utilize a variety of these methods/activities:

role playing   drill and practice   small group discussions

demonstrations

learning games

lectures with visual aids   mediated presentations (slide/tape, films, videotapes)   large group discussions

simulations

If lectures are necessary in your training sessions, allow for a one or two-minute break every 15 minutes. This gives the hearing-impaired members of the group time to relax their eyes.

Simplifying written materials

While not all hearing-impaired people have difficulty with reading, some do. For these people, try these techniques to modify printed training materials:

1. state the most important ideas first

2. introduce one idea or fact at a time

3. sequence ideas in order of occurrence

4. eliminate unnecessary words

5. select words which are commonly used by most people

6. break up long sentences into shorter ones

7. define technical terms and repeat information to ensure these terms can be understood

8. use simple, uncluttered illustrations

9. place illustrations close to the text they are to support and clearly label them

10. keep pronouns close to their referent

11. tie parts of sentences together with simple conjunctions (and, but, or)

12. whenever possible, place time and setting information at the beginning of the sentence

**Arranging the
classroom seating
(learning environment)**

When a speaker presents information, hearing people do
not have to see the speaker to understand the message.
Hearing-impaired people without much residual
(remaining) hearing depend upon their eyes to find out
what is being said. For most hearing-impaired people to
learn, they must be able to *see* all of the instruction that
is presented.

The classroom (learning environment) should be set up
so that *all* sources of visual information (including the
trainer, interpreter, blackboard, screen, etc.) are:

located where the
hearing-impaired
person can easily see
them

well lighted with no
sources of bright
light (like windows)
behind them

free from distractions
(people walking past,
curtains blowing,
etc.)

Keeping all sources of visual information in one fixed
location helps the hearing-impaired trainee know where
to look to get the information needed. This also saves
time because the trainer doesn't have to continuously
direct the hearing-impaired person's attention to other
places in the room.

Setting the trainees' expectations

It is important to begin a training session by telling the trainees:

what is going to happen

why it is important for this to occur

how this relates to them and their careers

By informing the group of the goals of the session and plans for working toward those goals, the trainer is preparing them to receive the instruction and motivating them to learn. This is especially important for a hearing-impaired trainee.

Evaluating trainee progress

Many training programs provide for testing of the trainee's knowledge at the end of each session or group of sessions. However, it is very important to evaluate the trainee's progress throughout the training period.

Most training sessions contain key points that trainees must learn before they will understand the next part of the training. When such points have been covered, pause and check the group's understanding of that material by:

asking people to summarize the major points which have been covered

requesting that the trainees ask any questions they might have about the material

asking for a show of hands in response to a question

calling on individuals to respond to questions (asked by you or other trainees)

Whenever possible, have trainees demonstrate a skill, rather than talk or write about it.

Managing communication in the classroom

In a classroom, all trainees need to know what others in the group are saying. Trainees learn from each other, as well as from the trainer. When all of the participants have normal hearing, they can listen easily to the thoughts, questions, and opinions of others. With a hearing-impaired person in the group, the trainer must ensure that the hearing-impaired person stays informed of what others are saying. Although this puts an added responsibility on the trainer, it is essential for the hearing-impaired person to be able to benefit fully from the training experience.

These simple procedures will ensure that all participants share equally in the communication that goes on in the classroom:

help other trainees understand what the hearing-impaired person said if his/her speech is hard to understand (the interpreter may be of assistance in doing this)

if the hearing-impaired person missed what was said, repeat it

acknowledge the speaker (point and/or say the person's name) so that the hearing-impaired person always knows who is speaking

allow time for the hearing-impaired person to look at the new speaker before the speaker begins

be sure that only one person talks at a time. A hearing-impaired person cannot listen to more than one person at once, and an interpreter, if used, can only interpret one speaker at a time

Helpful Hints
Here are some "helpful hints" for working with
hearing-impaired trainees in a variety of training
situations:

speak slowly and
clearly, but not in an
exaggerated way

become informed
about hearing losses,
their potential
impact, and hearing
aids

use visual aids
whenever possible

look directly at the
hearing-impaired
person. If your face
is hidden by objects,
or if you are facing
the blackboard, your
lips cannot be read

repeat and rephrase
any important points
and questions

seat the trainee
where he/she can see
the trainer,
interpreter (if used),
and all visual
information which
will be presented

work closely with
available
support people

periodically check
the trainee's
understanding of the
material being
presented

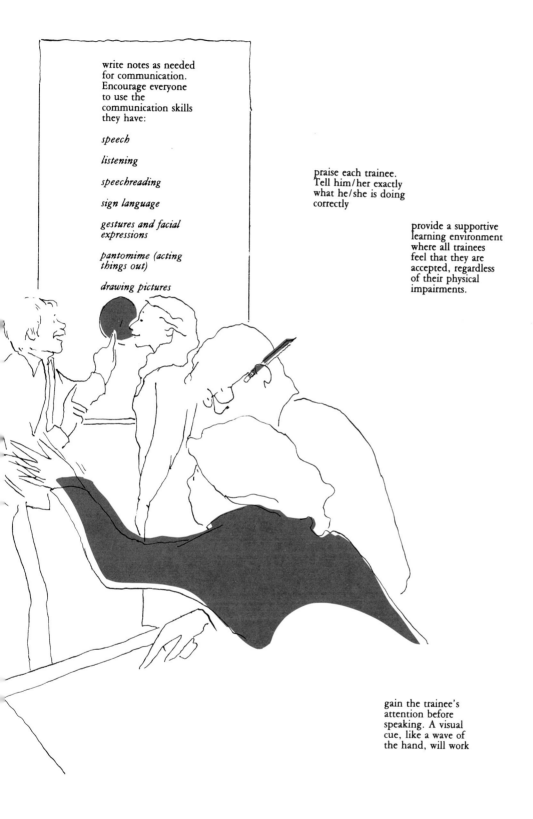

write notes as needed
for communication.
Encourage everyone
to use the
communication skills
they have:

speech

listening

speechreading

sign language

*gestures and facial
expressions*

*pantomime (acting
things out)*

drawing pictures

praise each trainee.
Tell him/her exactly
what he/she is doing
correctly

provide a supportive
learning environment
where all trainees
feel that they are
accepted, regardless
of their physical
impairments.

gain the trainee's
attention before
speaking. A visual
cue, like a wave of
the hand, will work

PART IV:

SUPPORT SERVICES:

Improving Job Performance

*"IBM has been trying to meet
my special needs, especially in
the area of communication.
Our secretary relays messages for
me through the TTY exchange
and I have a TTY."*

*"Once in a while I'll have
lunch with Bob, an electronic
technician. He's hearing
impaired, too."*

TYPES OF SUPPORT SERVICES

Being hearing impaired has consequences other than simply being unable to hear. It means facing communication barriers, either in giving and/or receiving verbal information.

For a hearing-impaired employee to receive the same information as a hearing counterpart, in training sessions and other group situations, specific support services may be appropriate, such as:

Interpreting using various methods to facilitate communication between hearing and hearing-impaired people

Notetaking recording information transmitted during group discussions, meetings, presentations, or training sessions

Tutoring reviewing/ clarifying information previously presented during a group event

COORDINATION OF SERVICES

When support services are provided, the need for a coordinating system arises. In any good system, the goal is balanced against the costs to achieve it. Some factors to consider when coordinating support services are:

number of hearing-impaired employees needing the service

communication skills of the hearing-impaired employee

communication requirements of the particular situation

communication skills of the hearing-impaired employee's co-workers

information needs and training of the hearing-impaired person's manager and co-workers

hearing-impaired employees' responsibilities regarding the use of these services

Some special services are better coordinated at the organizational level, while others can best be dealt with by the supervisor of the hearing-impaired employee. The responsibility of coordinating such services should be determined based on:

how often the service is required

the nature of the service

who is being served and how many are served at one time

how many people are involved in providing the service

other considerations unique to an organization, such as its size and internal structure

Services Which are Better Coordinated on an Organization-Wide Basis

It generally is a good idea to have organization-wide control over services which:

affect many people in the organization (both hearing and hearing impaired)

are *not* used regularly by a hearing-impaired individual within a single department

Some services which fall into this category are:

training of managers and co-workers, including additional guidance for managers, orientation to deafness seminars, and classes in sign language

inter-departmental communication networks, such as telecommunication devices to receive calls from hearing-impaired workers in other departments, and ordering and maintenance of telephone aids or signaling devices

interpreting services, if there is a need to use personnel across department lines or enough hearing-impaired employees to require a staff interpreter

Services Which are Better Coordinated on a Departmental Basis

It is preferable to have the hearing-impaired employee's supervisor control services which:

affect few people in the organization (for example, the hearing-impaired worker and a co-worker within the same department)

are used regularly by a single hearing-impaired individual

Some services which fall into this category are:

requesting an interpreter (if needed, and no one within the department can perform this function) for a group meeting

clarifying, for the hearing-impaired employee(s), what happened in the group meeting

asking someone to take notes at group meetings

circulation of written information of concern to the hearing-impaired employee(s) in the department

enforcing participation rules at group meetings

ensuring that meeting notes are distributed in a timely manner

securing telephone assistance for the hearing-impaired employee(s) (secretarial support and/or a device to use with the telephone)

Gaining Access to Support Services

Regardless of which level of the organization is given control over a support service, it is best if the hearing-impaired employee can quickly gain access to the support required with a minimal amount of involvement by others. Ultimately, it is the employee's responsibility to communicate what support services are needed to perform the job. To encourage this, it is helpful for a supervisor (or personnel representative) to discuss with the hearing-impaired employee what support services have been or could be made available. This exchange of information can help to clarify the individual's needs and the means by which they can be met.

INTERPRETING

WHAT IS INTERPRETING?

Hearing-impaired individuals use a variety of communication methods. Interpreters facilitate communication between hearing and hearing-impaired people by using these methods. They change spoken language into visual modes most easily understood by the hearing-impaired individual. Some of the frequently used methods include:

Manual Interpreting: the interpreter uses signs and fingerspelling. A variety of sign systems exist and the interpreter will use one which matches the style of the hearing-impaired person

Oral Interpreting: the interpreter, without using voice, mouths what the speaker says and uses techniques such as facial expressions and gestures to convey a message to the hearing-impaired speechreader

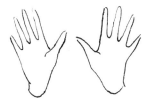

Oral-Manual Interpreting: the interpreter signs in English word order while mouthing the speaker's words

Voice or Reverse Interpreting: the interpreter says aloud the message of the hearing-impaired individual

WHEN AND WHERE SHOULD INTERPRETERS BE USED?

Interpreting services help some hearing-impaired people to better understand spoken information in large or small group situations. Interpreters may be used during:

pre-employment interviews

job performance appraisal sessions

large group meetings

special employee presentations

lectures and/or training seminars

The best judge of when an interpreter should be used is your hearing-impaired employee or job candidate. He/she knows when, and under what circumstances, interpreting services are helpful.

How to Arrange for Interpreting Services

To plan for situations in which you think an interpreter might be needed:

1. Inform your hearing-impaired employee or job candidate of the upcoming event.

2. Explain the purpose of the event, the type of information that will be presented and/or discussed, the length of the meeting, etc.

3. Determine if the employee or candidate wishes to have an interpreter. Others present might also find it helpful to have an interpreter in order to convey the hearing-impaired person's contributions to the discussion if an interpreter is required.

4. Ask the hearing-impaired employee or candidate if he/she knows of an interpreter or referral agency to contact.

5. If the hearing-impaired employee cannot recommend an individual or referral agency, use the listing of state and local Interpreter Referral Agencies provided in Appendix B. If a service is not listed for your community, contact the service closest to you. The people at that agency should be able to suggest to you whom to contact in your community, or consult the telephone directory for the local or state office of the:

- Registry of Interpreters for the Deaf (RID)
- State Office of Vocational Rehabilitation
- National Association of the Deaf (NAD)

**Things to Remember
When Using an
Interpreter**

1. If possible, notify the interpreter and/or interpreter referral service two to three weeks before the interpreting service is needed.

2. State the length of time the interpreter will be needed, the date, time of arrival, type of information to be presented, name and location of a contact person for the interpreter to meet upon arrival, and the type of interpreting required. The hearing-impaired employee(s) can tell you what type of interpreting will be needed.

3. If the material to be presented is highly technical or will be presented on a film, tape recorder, or videotape, inform the referral service or interpreter of this. The interpreter may need to bring along a light or may want to preview the material and/or talk with someone familiar with the content and vocabulary to make sure it is transmitted accurately.

4. Interpreters are paid on an hourly basis. Fees vary with the skill of the interpreter. Many times, due to the nature of the information being presented, the interpreter will need to be knowledgeable of the concepts and vocabulary in a specific technical area. Services then are priced accordingly. The Registry of Interpreters for the Deaf and/or the referral agency can tell you the current recommended fees for a particular type of service.

Rules for Hearing People
Using an Interpreter

1. Always talk directly to the hearing-impaired employee, not to the interpreter.

2. Allow the interpreter to sit or stand near the speaker. Make sure that the hearing-impaired members of the audience are seated where they can clearly see the message sent by the interpreter while also picking up cues from the speaker.

3. Provide a short break every hour or so. The interpreting process can be physically and mentally tiring for both the interpreter and the hearing-impaired person. Breaks help both people to function more effectively.

4. Do not ask an interpreter to interpret only selected portions of what is said. The interpreter follows a professional code of ethics which requires him/her to interpret everything that is said during a meeting. This code of ethics also prohibits the interpreter from sharing any information gained during an interpreting assignment. The interpreter is bound professionally to maintain confidentiality and impartiality.

5. Take time before the meeting to meet with the interpreter. There may be some vocabulary or acronyms which should be clarified for the interpreter. It also is helpful for both the interpreter and the hearing-impaired people in the group if the speaker uses overhead transparencies containing the special vocabulary or acronyms.

6. Depending on the type of interpreting being done, the interpreter may need to ask the speaker to slow down his/her rate of speech. If a slower speaking rate is required, the interpreter will say so. It also is helpful for the speaker to have some eye contact with the hearing-impaired audience members. The speaker thus can be alerted to times when he/she is speaking too fast. In general, the speaker should be able to maintain a ''normal'' speed for platform presentations.

7. Encourage the group to follow the rule that only one person will speak at a time. An interpreter can only accommodate one speaker at a time.

Placement of the Interpreter

Frequently an interpreter will arrive at an assignment to find the seating and lighting already arranged. It is helpful if those responsible for making seating/lighting arrangements are aware that an interpreter will be used and of the type of event. Appropriate arrangements then can be made using the following descriptions, thereby avoiding last minute changes and confusion.

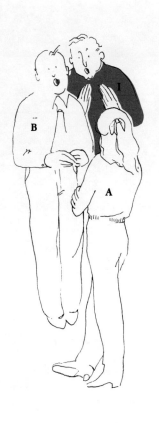

1. In a one-to-one situation, the interpreter sits or stands to the side and a little behind the hearing person.

A is the hearing-impaired person

B is the hearing person

I is the interpreter

2. In a training session or a classroom-type presentation, the interpreter should sit or stand so that the hearing-impaired employee can see the interpreter and any media that are being shown.

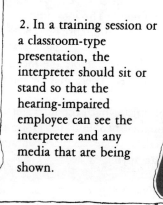

P is the presenter/instructor

I is the interpreter

A is/are the hearing-impaired members of the audience

3. If slides or a film is being shown during a training session, make sure there is a small spotlight, or some light, on the interpreter. The hearing-impaired employee cannot clearly see an interpreter's signs or mouthing in a dimly lighted area.

4. In a group discussion or meeting, seating should be arranged in a circle or semi-circle so all participants can be seen. The interpreter then can point to the person speaking.

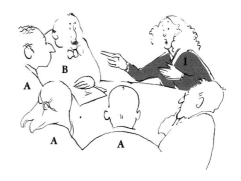

A is/are the hearing-impaired person(s)

B is the group leader or instructor (if there is one)

I is the interpreter

5. In large group presentations on a stage, the interpreter sits or stands to the side and slightly behind the speaker.

P is the presenter

I is the interpreter

A is/are the hearing-impaired members of the audience

REMEMBER:
In all interpreting situations, it is important that there be adequate lighting and a neutral or dark background behind the interpreter. This provides the best possible situation for the hearing-impaired person to see and understand the interpreter.

NOTETAKING

Because deafness is not a visible handicap, people often forget that it is difficult for a hearing-impaired employee to follow quick conversations, learn spoken lecture material, and/or follow long conversations. Hearing people also may forget that, to take notes during a meeting or training session, one must look away from the speaker and to the notes. This is difficult for a hearing-impaired person. Each time he/she looks away from the speaker (or interpreter) to take notes, some information is missed.

Current research suggests that what people *see* is not remembered or learned as well as what is *heard*. This means that even if a hearing-impaired person were watching an interpreter or a signing speaker, or were a skilled speechreader, he/she may not be able to recall all important information. This puts added importance on clear, complete notes.

The hearing-impaired employee can be assisted during group discussions and meetings, large group presentations, and training sessions by notetakers. The notetaker:

records as much information as possible

puts the notes into a logical order

highlights the main ideas

emphasizes the main topics

When a meeting or event ends, the notetaker gives the notes directly to the hearing-impaired person, who now has an opportunity to ask questions and/or have confusing points clarified by the notetaker or tutor.

It is not necessary to hire someone from outside the department or organization to take notes. Co-workers, other trainees, secretaries, or supervisors can learn to take notes for the hearing-impaired employee. It helps if someone familiar with the topics being discussed is the notetaker. The notes also could be used by others in the class or meeting, or by the instructor when evaluating or revising the course. The notes could be especially useful for employees who are not native English speakers or who have a physical handicap which affects language and writing ability.

How to Take Notes

The following principles should be used to guide the notetaker in performing his/her task.

Use only one side of the paper. This allows space for clarifying remarks, if needed.

Number, title, and date each page of the notes.

Use a black pen. It is easier to read and makes better photographic copies.

Write everything in complete sentences. Using sentence fragments and phrases can be confusing to the reader.

Notes do not have to be complete transcripts of every word that is spoken. A good, clear outline with major points and vocabulary (all in complete sentences) is better than a word-for-word record.

Write clearly and legibly. Make sure the hearing-impaired employee can read the notetaker's handwriting.

Leave blanks when unsure of the specific word, idea, or statement. The missing information can be gathered together and inserted after the session or meeting has ended.

Take notes as if the hearing-impaired person *did not attend* the event. Do not assume he/she knows or remembers something because of attendance at the event.

Use correct spelling.

Mark points to emphasize important ideas and/or concepts. Underline, CAPITALIZE, or enclose important points in a box.

Indicate the speaker, particularly when trainees are discussing things or asking the trainer questions. Be sure the trainer's responses are marked clearly.

Specific information about future meetings, classes, and outside responsibilities should be emphasized clearly in the notes.

Make sure abbreviations are understandable. Write words out the first few times so that the abbreviation is made clear. (i.e. "solid state" = s.s.)

Leave wide margins, indentations, and spaces between lines.

For additional information about notetaking, see the sources listed in Appendix C.

TUTORING

A large amount of verbal information can be presented during a group event. This volume of verbal information, combined with the difficulty hearing-impaired people have in processing spoken messages, makes tutoring a useful support service. Tutoring may be desirable immediately after small group meetings, training sessions, orientation seminars, or large group presentations.

The hearing-impaired person's tutor could be his/her notetaker, co-worker, interpreter, or another trainee (agreed upon in advance). The tutor serves not as a trainer but rather as someone helping a friend. The tutor may:

review the information previously presented

answer the hearing-impaired person's questions

supply missing information

clarify new vocabulary, procedures, forms, etc.

Rules for the Tutor

be encouraging and friendly. It may not be easy for the hearing-impaired person to admit that he/she does not understand something

work with the trainer and the hearing-impaired person to create a comfortable situation for all*

For additional information about tutoring, see the sources listed in Appendix C.

PART V:

AIDS FOR THE HEARING-IMPAIR

EMPLOYEE: Special Products and Equipment

"Sometimes I think this computer has a hearing problem, too!"

"My data processing instructor told me once that deaf people are like computers — it takes a little extra effort to learn how to communicate with them, but it's well worth it."

"I have received training via computer-assisted instruction (CAI), which really helped me a lot. CAI helps everybody learn faster — and for me, it was perfect. I was able to train on the same basis as my co-workers."

"The TTYs in my office and at home are great for talking to a variety of people. Many of the people I talk to on a regular basis have no idea that I'm deaf. Fortunately, and sometimes unfortunately, my boss can now reach me almost anywhere, even at home!"

ADAPTING AUDIOVISUAL MATERIALS

Severely hearing-impaired people cannot hear the sound track of a filmstrip, slide show, or videotape. Even hearing-impaired people who can hear the sound track may hear distorted or unclear sounds. For all practical purposes, assume that the sound track is not understandable for the hearing-impaired trainee.

Whenever you use training materials which have a sound track and provide training to a group of both hearing and hearing-impaired people, consider how best to accommodate the needs of the hearing-impaired person while providing the training needed by the entire group.

There are several ways to provide the hearing-impaired trainee with the information contained on a sound track. The following list identifies methods for adapting sound track material for hearing-impaired trainees.

**Methods for
Adapting Sound
Track Media**

	Advantages	*Disadvantages*
PRINTED SCRIPT	inexpensive easy to obtain	user can't look at script and visual at the same time
LIVE INTERPRETER	inexpensive but cost increases with use done more quickly than methods requiring product reproduction allows for explanations, if needed	interpreter must be scheduled each time materials are used user must look back and forth from interpreter to visuals
INTERPRETER SUPERIMPOSED ON MOVING VISUALS (film or videotape/disc)	moderately expensive materials can be used again without an interpreter being scheduled	covers part of the visual must obtain permission to change product requires time to modify product
CAPTIONS	preferred by most hearing-impaired people most understandable can be used by both hearing and hearing-impaired employees can be used by users and non-users of sign language	fairly expensive initially takes time must obtain permission to change product

Media Selection

When preparing to train hearing-impaired employees, it may be necessary to:

adapt existing in-house training materials

select externally produced training materials which already have been adapted

select externally produced training materials which can be adapted

In any of these situations, you will need to:

determine what is needed

find out about available products

select and/or adapt appropriate products

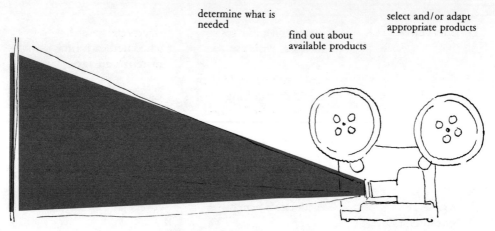

These tasks can be accomplished by following these steps:

1. Determine what the audience is like:

what skills do they already have in this training area?

what reading and writing skills do they have?

what interests?

what work experience?

2. Determine the objectives of the training:

Do you want to:	*So the trainees will:*
instruct	be able to do something?
motivate	want to do something?
inform	be able to talk about a particular area?
provide practice	have an opportunity to use a skill?
evaluate	be able to show how well they can do something?

Write your objectives so that it is clear what you want to be able to have the trainees do or say upon completion of the training.

3. Specify how many people will use the materials at one time:

large group   pairs

    small group   individuals

4. Locate materials to fit the training objectives and the audience's characteristics and size. Use resources to fit your goal, whether it is the selection of materials unadapted for use with hearing-impaired people or the selection of previously adapted materials.

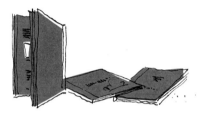

5. Review materials which have been located and selected on the basis of the special needs of hearing-impaired members of the training audience:

ideas and facts shown, not just talked about

sound track use of simple sentences written in a straight-forward manner

pace slow enough to read captions or interpreter's signs

background sound (not spoken words) containing no essential information

moderately paced sound track (on moving visuals)

limited talking between two or more people

limited number of changes between on and off-camera speakers

If you adapt a product for use with hearing-impaired people by:

copying the product and adding captions

editing part of the product

copying the product and superimposing an interpreter on the moving visuals

you must obtain permission from the copyright holder. Permission is *not* required when captions are put on slides to be projected *along with* the original media.

For more information, see Appendix D.

How to Obtain Copyright Permission

1. When copyright permission is required, contact the individual or group that holds the copyright. This usually is indicated by a name and date following the copyright symbol marked on the product.

2. Address the request to one of the following company representatives:

permissions officer   vice president

marketing manager   president

Although the distributor may not hold the rights to the product, the firm should be able to identify the holder of the rights.

3. After locating and contacting the copyright holder, explain the request, stating specifics such as:

number of copies to   plans for use and
be made   distribution
                    any visual and/or
                    verbal editing
                    desired

4. Secure permission and determine what fees, if any, are required.

5. Send a follow-up letter which confirms the request and permission previously agreed upon. Make sure that a copy of the letter is signed and returned by the copyright holder.

AUDIOVISUAL EQUIPMENT

When presenting audiovisual materials to a group of hearing and hearing-impaired people, certain techniques can be used to help the hearing-impaired audience members benefit from the presentation. Such techniques also may be beneficial to hearing audience members and will not interfere with the flow of information.

Using Audio Equipment
Some hearing-impaired people can gain access to information contained on a sound track or spoken by a person using a public address system. Before attempting to use any of the following equipment and techniques, it is best to ask your hearing-impaired employee if he/she would find it helpful. If your employee does not use a hearing aid, or finds it only marginally helpful, it is best to seat him/her as close as possible to the sound source. This helps the hearing-impaired person pick up both sounds and vibrations.

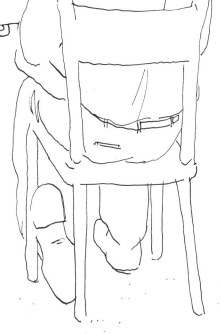

Audio Equipment and Techniques for Use with Hearing-Impaired Employees

PUBLIC ADDRESS SYSTEM

seat the hearing-impaired employee as close to the speakers as possible

use a normal volume setting

provide a notetaker or interpreter

TAPE RECORDERS/ PLAYERS

seat the hearing-impaired employee as close to the player as possible

provide a notetaker

some hearing-impaired people find it useful to tape and later play back presentations, if they can auditorily understand what was said

HEADPHONES (highly amplified)

place in auditoriums, theatres, and classrooms close to the presentation area

hearing-impaired people who are able to hear and understand speech fairly well often benefit from these units

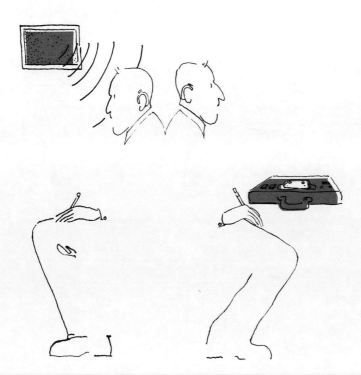

Inductive Loop System

This system is composed of:

a sound source

an amplifier

length of multi-conductor wire

hearing-impaired person using a hearing aid with a "T" (telephone) mode switch

The wire is looped around the area where the hearing-impaired person is seated. Any sound fed into the amplifier then can be picked up by the person's hearing aid when the switch is on the "T" setting. This system is limited by:

how much benefit each individual gets from a hearing aid

whether the hearing-impaired person has a hearing aid with a "T" switch

how many hearing-impaired people can fit inside the loop

The system, depending on its size, may be portable or permanent.

Wireless Frequency Modulated (FM) Listening System

This system is composed of:

an FM transmitter (microphone)

an FM receiver

headphones or an attachment to a person's hearing aid

The speaker (instructor/trainer/lecturer) wears a wireless FM transmitter (microphone) and the hearing-impaired person wears a wireless FM receiver. Because the speaker's voice is close to the transmitter (mike), the hearing-impaired person receives the voice as if he/she were listening at close range. Background noise is reduced to a minimum, something that does not happen using a hearing aid alone. The benefit derived from this system depends upon the listening skills of the user. The system is completely portable and there are several companies which manufacture this type of equipment for educational purposes.

VISUAL EQUIPMENT

Visuals provide perhaps the most effective method of sending information to a hearing-impaired person. However, many of the machines used to project visuals (film projectors, slide projectors, etc.) have fans and motors whose noise is in the range of frequencies amplified by most hearing aids. This results in a hearing-impaired person obtaining less information from a speaker or sound track than would otherwise be the case. This problem can be overcome by using a projection booth or a rear projection room. The following chart describes some pieces of visual equipment and ways you can use them to benefit your hearing-impaired employee.

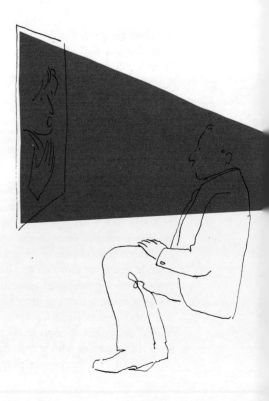

16mm FILM
PROJECTOR

35mm SLIDE
PROJECTOR

OVERHEAD
PROJECTOR

allow the hearing-
impaired person to sit
close to the screen with
projector at the rear of
the room to prevent
operating noise from
disturbing the person

allow the hearing-
impaired person to sit
near the screen; this
assures legible captions or
clear view of the
interpreter

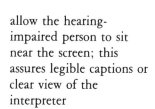

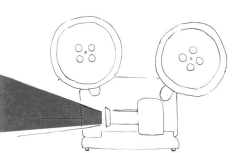

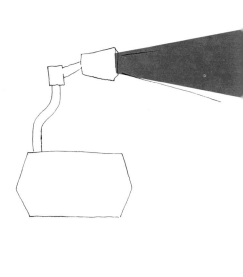

OVERHEAD PROJECTOR

FILMSTRIP PROJECTOR

usually the loudest of the visual projectors; seat the hearing-impaired person as far from the projector as possible

TELEVISION

seat the hearing-impaired person close enough to the screen to make captions legible; operating noise poses no problems

allow the hearing-impaired person to sit as close to the screen as possible; low operating noise usually does not pose problems

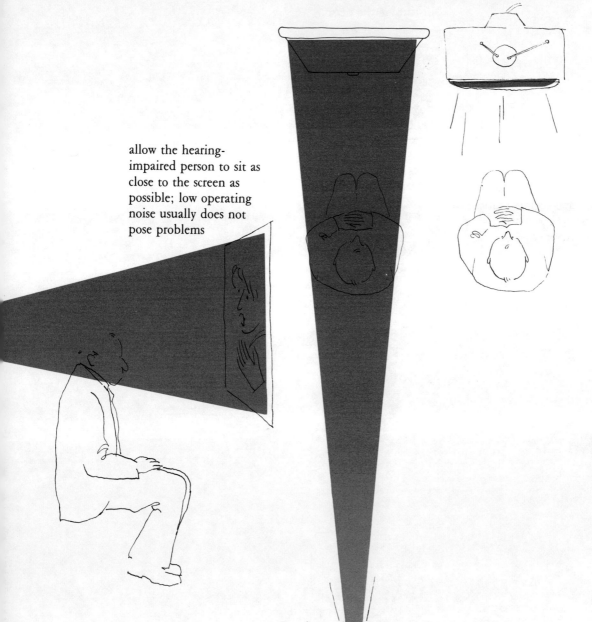

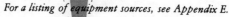

For a listing of equipment sources, see Appendix E.

TELEPHONES AND TELECOMMUNICATION DEVICES

Telephone Use by Hearing-Impaired People

Some hearing-impaired people are able to use the telephone. Whether or not a hearing-impaired individual can use the telephone depends upon:

the person's listening abilities

the person's speaking abilities

how familiar the person is with the topic of conversation

how familiar the person is with the speaker on the other end of the line

the telephone being used

Let's look at how each of these factors can affect a hearing-impaired person's ability to use the telephone.

Listening and Speaking Abilities

When two people have a telephone conversation, communication occurs only when each person is able to understand what the other is saying. Therefore, a hearing-impaired person using the telephone must be able to listen to and understand what the other person is saying. The speech of the hearing-impaired person also must be clear enough for the other person to understand it. Neither person can depend upon sign language, speechreading, facial expressions, or written messages while using the phone.

Familiarity with the Person Speaking

Hearing people sometimes are surprised when a hearing-impaired person carries on a telephone conversation with an old friend, but has difficulty talking with a stranger. Such differences occur because the hearing-impaired person has, with practice, become accustomed to the friend's speech pattern. It may take some time for the hearing-impaired person to understand the speech of someone new.

Familiarity with the Topic

All of us are better able to follow conversations when we are familiar with the topic being discussed. This is especially true for the hearing-impaired person. When hearing-impaired people communicate with others, they often have to guess about what has been said. The situation is comparable to taking a "fill-in-the-blank" test. You obviously would do better on the test if you studied the material covered on the test. Likewise, the hearing-impaired person's "guesses" about a conversation are more accurate when he/she is familiar with the words and ideas being discussed.

The Telephone Being Used

The volume at which the telephone's earpiece can transmit sound affects how well a hearing-impaired person can hear what the other person says. Most hearing-impaired telephone users need to have the transmitted sound made louder than normal. This can be done with a hearing aid with a standard telephone handset or an amplified telephone handset (with or without a hearing aid also being used).

Many hearing aids have a "T" setting designed to work with the magnetic leakage from telephone handsets. The handset must have a sufficient amount of leakage for this setting to be useful. The telephone company can provide a handset with the strong magnetic leakage needed to be compatible with this hearing aid setting.

A telephone can be amplified with a handset with a volume control built in, a portable amplifier which slips onto the handset, or an amplifier attached to a regular telephone.

The first method involves the telephone company replacing the standard handset with one which amplifies sound. Such an adaptation is particularly useful when a hearing-impaired person regularly uses the same telephone. On this type of handset, the volume control allows the volume to be set at a comfortable level for that individual.

When a person with normal hearing needs to use the telephone, the volume level can be adjusted to the usual level.

A portable amplifier is convenient for the hearing-impaired person who must use several different telephones. With this device, the battery powered amplifier slips over the handset and the volume is adjusted to suit the hearing-impaired person's needs. However, the portable amplifier may not be able to make the volume as loud as some hearing-impaired people need it to be.

An amplifier attached to a regular telephone makes it easier to discriminate between sounds and reduces static.

To make it possible for your hearing-impaired employee to use the telephone successfully:

determine what type of amplification system he/she finds most useful and appropriate and take steps to provide that system

identify someone who can make telephone calls for a hearing-impaired worker who cannot use the telephone or is confronted with a difficult telephoning situation

determine in what situations, if any, the hearing-impaired person regularly uses the telephone

Unless the hearing-impaired individual commonly uses the telephone in a variety of situations, his/her job should not involve regularly placing lengthy calls to strangers.

Telecommunication Devices

Telecommunication Devices for the Deaf (TDDs) make it possible for hearing-impaired people who cannot use an amplified telephone (due to speaking or listening problems) to communicate over a standard telephone. TDDs are made up of a typewriter-like keyboard, a telephone coupler, and some form of visual display. The visual display may be in the form of printed characters on paper, an alpha-numeric display (like the numbers on an electronic watch), or both.

The TDD user places a telephone handset on the coupler and types in the message he/she wishes to send. When a character on the keyboard is pressed to type in the message, a series of tones is generated. There is a different set of tones for each character. Those tones which form the typed message are sent over telephone lines to the telephone on the other end of the line. This telephone also must be linked to a TDD so that the message can be decoded and displayed.

A TDD allows a hearing-impaired person to send and receive telephone calls just as hearing employees would do. It is, of course, good for a hearing-impaired employee to experience the independence such telephone usage can provide. However, if contacting others within the organization via the telephone is an essential part of the hearing-impaired person's job, a TDD is more than simply a handy piece of equipment for an employer to provide. It becomes a tool which the employee needs to work effectively. Of course, for that person's TDD to be of use, there must be others at key locations within the organization.

The following chart summarizes some of the major factors to consider when purchasing TDDs from one of the more than 10 current manufacturers.

Purchasing Considerations

	Features	Type of Use	Cost	Reliability
PORTABLE MODELS	fewer choices than non-portable models	better for traveling or in small spaces	$300 to $750	reflected in price; generally not as good as non-portables
NON-PORTABLE MODELS	more choices than portable models; select on basis of what is needed	can only be used in one location and require more space	$700 to $2,000	reflected in price; generally better than portables

Almost all units come with a one-year warranty. If repairs are needed, units usually have to be sent back to the factory. Some non-portable units can be purchased with an optional maintenance contract. Often, local service people can repair non-portables.

Hi-Line Services

In some communities, a special free communication service is available to hearing-impaired telephone users. The service, sometimes called "Hi-Line," makes it possible for a hearing-impaired person, using a TDD, to contact a hearing person who has a telephone. The hearing-impaired person dials the Hi-Line on a TDD. The Hi-Line operator on duty reads the teletyped message and relays the information to the hearing person on another telephone. The operator then relays the message from the hearing person back to the hearing-impaired caller via a TDD. The Hi-Line service thus can form a vital communication link between the hearing-impaired person and the community.

To find out about the availability of such a service in your community, contact the Office of Vocational Rehabilitation or the United Way in your area.

SIGNALING
DEVICES

Hearing people are accustomed to having alarms, bells, sirens, buzzers, and beeps alert them to things happening around them. In the workplace, they may hear telephones ringing, pagers beeping, timers buzzing, fire alarms blaring, or horns honking. But how can hearing-impaired employees be alerted to the events occurring around them?

The simplest way to ensure that a hearing-impaired employee is informed of an emergency (as in the case of a fire) is to use a buddy system. With this method, a hearing worker is assigned to the hearing-impaired employee. He/she then is responsible for getting the hearing-impaired person away from the source of danger.

The buddy system is an effective method for emergencies. However, for routine events, this system requires too much of the hearing person's time. For this reason, signaling devices are available to inform hearing-impaired people of daily events that require their attention.

Signaling devices produce visual signals and/or vibrations that supplement auditory signals. These devices can be used to signal:

ringing telephones   machine malfunctions   knocks on the door

beeping pagers

ringing doorbells   smoke/fire alarms

There are two types of signaling devices: single purpose and multi-purpose.

Single Purpose
One example of a single purpose device is a desk lamp plugged into a special telephone signaler. When the telephone rings, the desk lamp flashes on and off. Another single purpose device is a vibrating pager. The Federal Communication Commission has set aside radio frequencies for use with vibrating pagers for hearing-impaired people.

Multi-Purpose
Multi-purpose devices respond to different sounds occurring in a room. Since the visual signals can match the distinctive rhythm pattern of a sound, it is possible for the hearing-impaired person to determine where to direct his/her attention.

Signaling devices often can easily be incorporated into an existing alarm or paging system. In most cases, the cost of such devices ranges from $50-$200.

The following are some practical tips on how you can help make the workplace safer and more convenient for the hearing-impaired employee and his/her co-workers:

Safety Tips

Set up a buddy system for dealing with emergency situations. Such a system could be used with all employees, not only hearing-impaired employees

Determine which sounds in the hearing-impaired employee's environment need to be translated into visual signals or vibrations. Both the hearing-impaired person's safety and working efficiency should be considered when determining what signaling devices are needed

Contact distributors of signaling devices for the hearing impaired. Assess available products on the basis of the employee's needs, as well as available features and prices

Inform the hearing-impaired person about what signaling devices are to be installed, and when and how each one works

Make sure that once devices have been installed, they are checked regularly for proper functioning. This is most important for signals attached to alarms

In some jobs, a hearing-impaired person may work in an area in which a leak in a gas line could occur. Normally, such leaks are detected by the sound of escaping gas. For the safety of the hearing-impaired employee and his/her co-workers, an easily detected odor can be added to the lines to make it possible for all employees to detect this source of danger

In work locations which lack a fail-safe system, small, fail-safe, plug-in lights can be used. When such lights are available during power failures, the hearing-impaired employee can see well enough to receive information. All employees could benefit from the availability of such lights in emergencies

When a hearing-impaired employee works at night or during off hours (weekends, holidays, etc.), security people in the building should be notified. The area where the hearing-impaired person is working should be checked regularly to be sure that he/she is in no danger

PART VI:

THE HEARING-IMPAIRED EMPLO

E: A Recognized Asset

"Someday I'm going to design a microprocessor for my hearing aid that will re-word everything to my liking. 'The Yankees lost the game' would come out, 'The Yankees won the game!' "

PROFILES

The following profiles illustrate that hearing-impaired employees are as competent, technically qualified, hard working, and cooperative as their hearing counterparts.

All capable, motivated employees — regardless of their hearing abilities — seek the challenges, rewards, and career mobility associated with superior job performance. Such people require only the opportunity to prove themselves to be valuable members of the work force.

William Schwall
Telephone Installer
Southwestern Bell

William ''W.O.'' Schwall is a hearing-impaired person in a non-traditional job — he is a telephone installer for Southwestern Bell. One of the people responsible for this daring hiring decision was a blind personnel officer who believes disabled people should focus on what they *have* rather than on what they *lack*.

W.O. was hired in 1978. He was the first deaf or hearing person who was able to meet the rigid requirements established for the job. After being interviewed, he was found to be capable, creative, assertive, determined to succeed, and outgoing and friendly.

The content of W.O.'s training remained the same as that of other trainees: lectures, demonstrations, and self-instruction. The only modifications for W.O. were an interpreter and a written script of some audio cassettes. In addition to translating spoken words into sign language, his interpreter also provided tutoring and short explanations when required. (Interpreters do not usually provide tutoring.)

W.O.'s supervisory personnel and training team worked together to identify problem areas W.O. might encounter, including communication with customers, communication with other departments at Southwestern Bell, and telephone testing and diagnostic problems with existing phones.

Cards were printed identifying W.O., his job, and adding, "PLEASE SHOW ME WHAT YOU WANT ME TO DO." He also was given a message pad. He soon found that the pad was all he needed to communicate with the customers.

Telecommunication Devices for the Deaf (TDDs) were purchased for W.O., including a Porta Printer for the main office and a pocket-size TDD. With these units, he could reach the home office, which could relay messages to other areas.

The challenge of telephone testing and diagnosis was addressed by an amateur inventor who developed a test device which translated sounds (dial tone, ringing, etc.) into light signals.

Many things have contributed to W.O.'s five years of success on the job. Management is supportive, supervisors meet with him regularly to discuss progress, co-workers attend sign language classes, customers respond positively, and W.O. works hard to overcome problems.

Tom Coughlan
Biomedical Photographer
Yale University School of Medicine

Twenty-six-year-old Tom Coughlan was the first deaf graduate of the biomedical photographic communications program at Rochester Institute of Technology. In June 1979, immediately upon graduation, he found a job — not only in his field, but at the prestigious School of Medicine at Yale University in New Haven, Connecticut.

He taught his co-workers to sign, despite the fact that he had learned sign language only a few years before as a student. Although he has "broken the sound barrier" within his office, Coughlan still encounters subtle discrimination on the job.

"Often," he explains, "doctors come into the lab to make a request or discuss photographs we have taken. When they see me, and realize I'm deaf, their first question is, 'May I please speak with a photographer?' " Nonetheless, his co-workers seem to have taken to him as much as he has to them.

Virginia Simon, director of the department of medical illustration and photography, says she did not know Coughlan was deaf when she received his resume, and that he was hired because of his excellent qualifications for the job.

"However," she recalls, "he did note on his resume that he had worked with deaf children, and that influenced my perception of him ahead of time. I think that by having Tom work with us we become aware of the small and subtle ways in which deaf persons are discriminated against daily — the little things — and I think it's important for us, as human beings, to know about that."

Coughlan's immediate supervisor is Patrick Lynch, who notes that working with a deaf person requires little effort.

"Tom functions so well in the hearing world that you're not acutely aware that he is deaf," he says. "There are some things that you naturally adapt to — not speaking with him unless he is looking at you, for example."

Another co-worker is office secretary Arlene Resnick, who learned fingerspelling and enough sign language so that she can competently negotiate telephone conversations for Coughlan.

Coughlan's photography partner, Randall Smith, notes, "The only problem we have is trying to talk while working together in the darkroom, because of the lighting. Maybe it's compensation, but his performance as a photographer is better than most."

Anne Makler
Staff Accountant
J.C. Penney

Anne Makler joined J.C. Penney as a staff accountant in 1978. She was the first hearing-impaired associate in the Controller's Department. Her supervisor says that her deafness has never interfered with her work.

"Most people who work with Anne can communicate with her very well," says Bill Wilhelms, who recalls unconsciously shouting at Makler when he interviewed her for the job. Shouting, he soon learned, was unnecessary, since Makler is proficient at reading lips and speaks as well.

"When people met me for the first time, they didn't know how to talk to me," Makler recalls. Fellow associates didn't realize, for example, that to enable Makler to read their lips they had to look directly at her. In addition, anything that obscures lip movements, such as mustaches, beards, or hands in front of a speaker's face, also interferes with her ability to read lips.

Soon, however, co-workers learned how to make themselves understood. And Makler strengthened her communication skills by taking a "Let's Write Well" course with other associates at her level. The course helped build her letter and memo-writing skills.

Makler is unable to use the telephone, so a co-worker answers her phone and talks on her behalf. She uses a TDD with the phone to transmit and receive messages from other hearing-impaired people using the same device.

To improve her professional skills, Makler completed course requirements for a certificate in Management Accounting, using an interpreter who translated the instructor's words into American Sign Language for her. This support service enabled Makler to take notes and ask questions.

She says that she would like to see more hearing-impaired people working at J.C. Penney. "I was the first deaf person in the department. I hope I can open the door for others."

Andrea Kurs
Visual Information Specialist
Naval Air Systems Command

Andrea Kurs is the first hearing-impaired person ever to work for the Naval Air Systems Command (NAVAIR) in Washington, D.C. As a visual information specialist, she produces viewgraphs (overhead transparencies) for use in formal presentations.

Kurs' co-workers describe her as an exceptionally pleasant, hard-working employee. Last year she earned an award for superior performance. Her supervisor says, "She sticks to whatever you give her and does a good, accurate job with a minimum of extra instruction."

Kurs finds communication with others at work to be no problem. She often writes notes on a small pad at her drafting table, and has been speechreading since age 4. For telephone communication, she uses a Teletypewriter (TTY). For calls which require speaking to non-TTY-equipped numbers, Kurs asks a friend or uses one of several local hotlines for the hearing impaired.

In conjunction with another hearing-impaired NAVAIR employee, Kurs teaches a lunchtime sign language course for her co-workers. Currently from five to eight students meet weekly for 45 minutes of instruction in American Sign Language.

Kurs is active in community affairs, is vice president of NTID's Metropolitan Washington, D.C., alumni chapter, and enjoys many sports. Her future plans? To work as an educational specialist or in a publications position. Her disability definitely has not limited her services to NAVAIR. Her supervisor says, "I wish I had a dozen more like her."

ENSURING EMPLOYEE SUCCESS ON THE JOB

Many prospective employers may be concerned that hiring a hearing-impaired employee will necessitate the purchase of costly equipment. These profiles indicate that this usually is not the case. The most commonly required equipment purchase is a TDD. Prospective employers also are concerned with the added burden that a hearing-impaired employee will place upon a supervisor. Supervisors, however, express satisfaction with most hearing-impaired employees' abilities to adapt to the work environment. Many talk with pride of the success they have shared with their hearing-impaired employees.

Acceptance of the hearing-impaired employee by supervisors and co-workers can be facilitated through workshops or seminars on deafness and its potential effects on the individual. Participants in such events should be told that hearing-impaired individuals vary in their communication skills and needs. During the hearing-impaired person's first days on the job, fellow employees can determine which communication strategies meet the needs of everyone in the work area. Everyone should remember that patience and a cooperative group spirit can go a long way in assisting the hearing-impaired employee to become a productive team member.

The following steps should be taken when considering placing a hearing-impaired (or otherwise disabled) employee in your organization.

1. *Win commitment to the idea from upper-level management.* Equal Employment Opportunities regulations provide only part of the story. Beyond compliance with external rules, an organization's managers must recognize the contribution which can be made by employees with varied backgrounds, skills, and abilities. Commitment from the top can influence the lower-level commitment that is needed for success.

2. *Determine the true requirements for the job —
physical, mental, and emotional.* Too often, disabled
employees are kept out of a job because of a job
description that reflects the skills and abilities of those
who previously have held the position, rather than those
which are essential to performing the job. Once the
necessary skills and abilities are defined for a job, the
pool of potentially qualified candidates may become
larger.

3. *Select a competent, technically qualified candidate.*
The candidate for the job should possess, or demonstrate
the capacity to acquire, those essential skills and abilities
noted in the job description. Irrelevant attributes should
not be used to screen out otherwise appropriate
candidates. By the same token, unqualified applicants,
regardless of their special circumstances, should not be
considered. The hiring of unqualified people eventually
will close the door to those people of similar
circumstance who are indeed qualified for a position.

4. *Plan for cooperation among team members in the
anticipation and solving of problems.* People who will
work with a disabled employee should be informed
about that person's skills, abilities, and needs before
his/her arrival on the job. Through orientation seminars
and group meetings, those most able to foresee
problems and suggest solutions will be able to provide
valuable input. The disabled employee's acceptance on
the job can be facilitated when co-workers and
supervisors are given the opportunity to ask and answer
questions and thereby become involved in that
employee's successful placement.

5. *Modify training to meet the special needs of the
trainee.* Training programs should be reviewed to
determine those aspects of the program which are
essential to the trainee's success on the job. Essential
instruction should then be modified to meet the needs
of the special trainee. This usually means a change in
the form of delivery rather than in the instruction itself.
The standards for successful completion of training
should not be lowered for the special trainee, providing
the standards accurately reflect what is required on the job.

6. *Provide the employee with the tools for success.*
Sometimes a piece of equipment will need to be
adapted, enhanced, or replaced to meet the needs of a

particular employee. At other times, support devices (provided by fellow employees or outside sources) are needed. Regardless of the type of tool needed, the employee should not be expected to perform a task when necessary elements for success have not been provided or the job has not been adjusted to accommodate these missing elements.

7. *Actively supervise the employee.* Employees need to know that their contributions to the organization are valuable. They also must be told how their efforts can be improved. If a supervisor does not give feedback to his/her employees, they will experience little job satisfaction and demonstrate limited improvement in their output. Disabled employees need the same supervision as other employees. They do not need protection from criticism or the silence of indifference.

8. *Expect the same quality of work from all employees.* Employees need to have their individual differences recognized. However, everyone who performs the same job should be expected to achieve the same level of proficiency. By maintaining the same standards for all employees within a job category, no one can complain that unfair advantages or disadvantages were given to an employee on the basis of his/her unique circumstances.

Appendix A

SCHOOLS FOR THE DEAF OR SCHOOLS WITH PROGRAMS FOR THE DEAF

There are many postsecondary programs in the United States which serve hearing-impaired persons. The programs listed here have a director assigned to the program for deaf persons, are accredited, offer a full range of support services for deaf students, and have at least 15 full-time deaf students enrolled.

Federally Established National Programs

Gallaudet College, District of Columbia
National Technical Institute for the Deaf at Rochester Institute of
    Technology, New York

Federally Established Regional Programs

California State University, Northridge, California
Delgado Community College, Louisiana
Seattle Central Community College, Washington
St. Paul Technical Vocational Institute, Minnesota

Other U.S. Postsecondary Programs

Alabama Institute for Deaf and Blind, Alabama
American River College, California
Arizona State University, Arizona
Bakersfield College, California
Birmingham Bible School for the Deaf, Alabama
California State Polytechnic University, Pomona, California
Catonsville Community College, Maryland
Central Bible College, Maryland
Central Piedmont Community College, North Carolina
Cerritos Community College, California
Chattanooga State Technical Community College, Tennessee
Chemeketa Community College, Oregon
Christ for the Nations Institute, Texas
City Colleges of Chicago, Illinois
College of Southern Idaho, Idaho
College of the Sequoias, California
Columbus Technical Institute, Ohio
Community College of Allegheny County, Boyce Campus,
    Pennsylvania
Community College of Denver, Colorado
Community College of Philadelphia, Pennsylvania
Cypress College, California
East Carolina University, North Carolina
East Central Oklahoma State University, Oklahoma
Eastfield College, Texas
El Camino College, California

El Camino Community College, California
Florida Junior College at Jacksonville, Florida
Florida State University, Florida
Floyd Junior College, Georgia
Gardner-Webb College, North Carolina
Golden West College, California
Howard County Junior College District-Southwest Collegiate Institute
    for the Deaf, Texas
Imperial Valley Community College, California
Iowa Western Community College, Iowa
J. Sargeant Reynolds Community College, Virginia
Johnson County Community College, Kansas
La Guardia Community College, New York
Laney College, California
Lenoir-Rhyne College, North Carolina
Lexington Technical Institute, Kentucky
Long Island University, New York
Los Angeles Pierce College, California
Madonna College, Michigan
Maryville College, Tennessee
Metropolitan Technical Community College, Nebraska
Michigan State University, Michigan
Mid-Florida Technical Institute, Florida
Milwaukee Area Technical College, Wisconsin
Mira Costa College, California
Mott Community College, Michigan
Mount Aloysius Junior College, Pennsylvania
New Hampshire Vocational Technical College at Claremont,
    New Hampshire
New River Community College, Virginia
North Central Technical Institute, Wisconsin
Northern Essex Community College, Massachusetts
Northern Illinois University, Illinois
Northwestern Connecticut Community College, Connecticut
Ohlone College, California
Pasadena City College, California
Pima Community College, Arizona
Pinellas Vocational Technical Institute, Florida
Portland Community College, Oregon
Riverside City College, California
San Antonio College, Texas
San Diego Mesa College, California
San Diego City College, California
San Jose Community College District, California
Santa Rosa Junior College, California
Southern Illinois University at Carbondale, Illinois
Spokane Falls Community College, Washington
St. Louis Community College at Florissant Valley, Missouri
St. Mary's Junior College, Minnesota
St. Petersburg Junior College, Florida
State Technical Institute and Rehabilitation Center, Minnesota
Stephen F. Austin State University, Texas
Tampa Technical Institute, Florida
Tarrant County Junior College District, Texas
Tennessee Temple University, Tennessee
Texas State Technical Institute, Texas
University of California, Riverside, California
University of Minnesota, Twin Cities Campus, Minnesota
University of Southern Colorado, Colorado
Washington State University, Washington
Washington University, Maryland
Waubonsee Community College, Illinois
West Valley Occupational Center, California
Western Oregon State College, Oregon
Western Piedmont Community College, North Carolina
William Rainey Harper College, Illinois

Canadian Postsecondary Programs

Alberta College, Alberta
Alberta Vocational Centre, Alberta
Atlantic Technological Vocational Centre, Nova Scotia
George Brown College of Applied Arts & Technology, Ontario
Red River Community College, Manitoba
Vancouver Community College — King Edward Campus, British
 Columbia

Additional Graduate Programs for Deaf Students

New York University, New York
University of Arizona, Arizona
University of Maryland, Maryland
Western Maryland College, Maryland

Rehabilitation and Adult Basic Education Programs

Jefferson State Vocational-Technical School, Kentucky
Los Angeles Trade-Technical College, California
Woodrow Wilson Rehabilitation Center, Virginia

More complete information on these programs can be found in

College and Career Programs for Deaf Students, available from:

Gallaudet College
Center for Assessment and Demographic Studies
Kendall Green
Washington, D.C. 20002

Appendix B

INTERPRETING RESOURCES

Central Office for
  Interpreter Services
Registry of Interpreters
  for the Deaf, Inc.
814 Thayer Avenue
Silver Spring, MD 20910
(301) 588-2406

Alabama

Deaf Interpreter & Referral Center
School of Public & Allied Health
University of Alabama, Birmingham
Birmingham, AL 35294
(205) 934-3323 (Voice or TDD)

Arizona

Community Outreach Program for
  the Deaf
3200 North Los Altos
Tucson, AZ 85705
(602) 888-0023

Valley Center of the Deaf
Interpreter Service Program
1016 North 32nd Street
Phoenix, AZ 95008
(602) 257-1921

California

Catholic Social Services
2869 Bush Street
San Francisco, CA 94115
(415) 567-0540 (Voice or TDD)

Community Center on Deafness
West Canon Perdido
202B Canon Perdido
Santa Barbara, CA 93101
(805) 965-6198 (Voice or TDD)

Community Council for the Deaf
343 East Main Street, Room 414
Stockton, CA 95202
(209) 948-1200 (Voice or TDD)

Dayle McIntosh Center
8100 Garden Grove Boulevard
Garden Grove, CA 92644
(714) 898-9571 (Voice)
(714) 892-7070 (TDD)

Deaf Community Services of
  San Diego
601 Market Street
San Diego, CA 92101
(714) 234-6666 (Voice)
(714) 234-1391 (TDD)

Deaf Counseling, Advocacy, &
  Referral Agency
3100 Mowry Avenue, Room 410
Fremont, CA 94538
(415) 794-0774 (Voice)
(415) 794-0777 (TDD)

Deaf Counseling, Advocacy, &
  Referral Agency
300 First Street, Room 234
San Jose, CA 95113
(408) 298-6770 (Voice)
(408) 298-5443 (TDD)

Deaf Counseling, Advocacy, &
  Referral Agency
1320 Webster Street
Oakland, CA 94612
(415) 465-9552 (Voice or TDD)

Greater L.A. Council on Deafness
Orange County Outreach
2024 North Broadway, Suite 109
Santa Ana, CA 90706
(714) 972-3925 (Voice or TDD)

Greater L.A. Council on Deafness
San Fernando Valley Outreach
14349 Hamlin
Van Nuys, CA 91401
(213) 785-5411 (Voice or TDD)

Greater L.A. Council on Deafness
San Gabriel Valley Outreach
8780 East Valley Boulevard
San Gabriel, CA 91770
(213) 573-3322 (Voice or TDD)

Greater L.A. Council on Deafness
South Central Outreach
8522 South Broadway
Los Angeles, CA 90003
(213) 753-1414 (Voice or TDD)

NorCal Center on Deafness
2755 Cottage Way, Suite 6
Sacramento, CA 95825
(916) 486-8570 (Voice or TDD)

Colorado

Center on Deafness
2120 South Holly Street, Room 105
Denver, CO 80222
(303) 758-1123

Pikes Peak Regional Center
 on Deafness
33 North Institute Street
Colorado Springs, CO 80903
(303) 634-2745 (Voice or TDD)

Valley Human Resources, Inc.
Greenhorn Valley Bank Building
P.O. Box 512
Colorado City, CO 81019
(303) 676-4080 (Voice)
(303) 676-3200 (TDD)

Connecticut

Commission on Deaf & Hearing
 Impaired
40 Woodland Street
Hartford, CT 06105
(203) 566-7414 (Voice or TDD)

Delaware

Deaf Contact
P.O. Box 3574
Wilmington, DE 19807
(302) 656-6660

District of Columbia

Interpreter Referral Center
Gallaudet College
Florida & Seventh Avenue N.E.
Washington, DC 20002
(202) 651-5634 (Voice or TDD)

Project Access
Deafpride, Inc.
2010 Rhode Island Avenue N.E.
Washington, DC 20018
(202) 635-2433

Florida

Deaf Services Bureau
4800 West Flagler Street
Suite 213
Miami, FL 33134
(305) 444-2266 (Voice)
(305) 444-2211 (TDD)

Deaf Services Bureau
6507 Sunset Strip
Sunrise, FL 33313
(305) 742-3240

Georgia

Georgia Registry of Interpreters for
 the Deaf
250 Georgia Avenue, S.E.
Room 211, Atlanta, GA 30312
(404) 524-2862

Hawaii

Information & Referral Center
1150 South King Street, Room 201
Honolulu, HA 96814
(808) 523-9144

Idaho

College of Southern Idaho
P.O. Box 1238
Twin Falls, ID 93301
(208) 733-9554 (Voice or TDD)

Illinois

Chicago Hearing Society
6 East Monroe Street
Chicago, IL 60603
(312) 332-6850

Indiana

Community Services Agency for the Deaf
1405 Broad Ripple Avenue
Indianapolis, IN 46220
(317) 259-7115

Community Services for Adult Deaf
United Health Services
711 East Colfax
South Bend, IN 46617
(219) 234-3136

Deaf Awareness & Interpreters of
 Northwest Indiana
8143 Kennedy Avenue
Highland, IN 46322

Deaf Social Service Agency for
 the Tri-State Inc.
312 Northwest 7th Street, Suite 203
Evansville, IN 47708
(812) 425-2726 (Voice)
(812) 425-2841 (TDD)

Northwest Indiana Service Agency
3680 179th Street, Suite C
Hammond, IN 46375
(219) 845-7110

Iowa

Deaf Services of Iowa
Lucas State Office Building
Des Moines, IA 50319
(515) 281-5343 (Voice or TDD)
(515) 281-3561 (after hours)

Kentucky

Kentucky Registry of Interpreters
608 Penquin Street
Louisville, KY 40217
(606) 588-4136

Rehabilitation Services for the Deaf
122 North Third Street
Danville, KY 40422
(606) 236-7767

Louisiana

Catholic Deaf Center
2585 Brightside Drive
Baton Rouge, LA 70808
(504) 766-9320

Maine

Pine Tree Society for Crippled
  Children and Adults
40 Woodmont Street
Portland, ME 04102
(207) 774-9438

Maryland

Deaf Referral Service
3312 Elmora Avenue
Baltimore, MD 21213
(301) 276-3323

Massachusetts

Massachusetts Office of Deafness
20 Providence Street
Boston, MA 02116
(617) 727-5106 (Voice)
(617) 727-5236 (TDD)

Michigan

Detroit Hearing & Speech Center
19185 Wyoming
Detroit, MI 48221
(313) 341-1353

Michigan Association for
  Better Hearing & Speech
724 East Abbot Road
East Lansing, MI 48823
(517) 337-1646 (Voice or TDD)

Social Services for the Hearing Impaired
1221 Beach Street
Flint, MI 48502
(313) 239-3112

Minnesota

Interpreter Referral Service
Minnesota Foundation for
  Better Hearing & Speech
518 Bremer Building
7th and Roberts Streets
St. Paul, MN 55101
(612) 222-6866 (Voice or TDD)

Mississippi

Community Services Program
Mississippi School for the Deaf
1253 Eastover Drive
Jackson, MS 39211
(601) 366-7154

De l'Epee Deaf Center
217 Cowan Road
Gulfport, MS 39501
(601) 896-6161

Missouri

Central Missouri
  Registry of Interpreters
  for the Deaf
Missouri School for the Deaf
5th and Vine Streets
Fulton, MO 65251
(314) 642-3301

St. Louis Registry of
  Interpreters for the Deaf
P.O. Box 311
Florissant, MO 63035
(314) 725-3837 (7 a.m.-10 p.m.)
(314) 725-5252 (10 p.m.-7 a.m.)

Montana

Montana School for the Deaf
3911 Central Avenue
Great Falls, MT 59401
(406) 453-1401

Services to the Deaf
Social & Rehabilitative Services
1818 10th Avenue, South, Suite 5
Great Falls, MT 59405
(406) 727-7740

New Hampshire

Communication Bridge
110 North Main Street
Manchester, NH 03301
(603) 669-5400

New Jersey

Registry Referral Service
1033 Springfield Avenue
Cranford, NJ 07016
(201) 272-8840

New Mexico

Interpreter Referral & Information
  Center
127 La Veta N.E.
Albuquerque, NM 87108
(505) 266-1073 (Voice)
(505) 255-8134 (TDD)

New York

Central New York Association for
  the Hearing Impaired
620 South Salina Street
Syracuse, NY 13202
(315) 422-2321 (Voice)
(315) 422-9746 (TDD)

Genesee Valley Registry
  of Interpreters for the Deaf
Community Referral Service
P.O. Box 23672
Rochester, NY 14692
(716) 436-3026

LaGuardia Community College
Interpreter Referral
31-10 Tomson Avenue
Long Island City, NY 11101
(212) 626-2705 (Voice)
(212) 392-9240 (TDD)

New York Society for the Deaf
Interpreter Service
344 East 14th Street
New York, NY 10003
(212) 673-6500 (Voice)
(212) 673-6974 (TDD)

New York University
Deafness Research & Training Center
80 Washington Square East
New York, NY 10003
(212) 598-2306

Service Bureau for the Deaf
P.O. Box 263
Nesconset, Long Island, NY 11767
(516) 265-8093 (8 a.m.-4:30 p.m.)
(516) 265-3885 (evenings/weekends)

Westchester County Office for
the Disabled
950 County Office Building
White Plains, NY 10601
(914) 682-3062 (Voice)
(914) 682-3408 (TDD)

Western New York Registry
of Interpreters for the Deaf
St. Mary's School for the Deaf
2253 Main Street
Buffalo, NY 14214
(716) 834-6838

North Carolina

Asheville Regional Community Service
Center for the Hearing Impaired
58 Grove Street
Asheville, NC 28801
(704) 258-2762

Charlotte Regional Community Service
Center for the Hearing Impaired
316 East Morehead Street, Room 308
Charlotte, NC 28204
(704) 334-1687 (Voice)
(704) 334-3481 (TDD)

Greenville Regional Community
Services Center for the Hearing
Impaired
223 West 10th Street, Room 142
Greenville, NC 27834
(919) 758-7557 (Voice or TDD)

Guildford County Communication
Center for the Deaf
1601 Walker Avenue
P.O. Box 5583
Greensboro, NC 27403
(919) 275-8878 (Voice or TDD)

Raleigh Regional Community Services
Center for the Hearing Impaired
4 Maiden Lane
Raleigh, NC 27607
(919) 733-6714 (Voice or TDD)

Winston-Salem Deafness Center
2701 North Cherry Street
Winston-Salem, NC 27105
(919) 724-3621

Ohio

Community Information Referral Service
370 South 5th Street
Columbus, OH 43215
(614) 221-9900 (Voice)
(614) 463-1122 (TDD)

Community Service for Deaf and
Hard-of-Hearing
Cleveland Hearing & Speech Center
11206 Euclid Avenue
Cleveland, OH 44106
(216) 231-8787 (Voice)
(216) 721-4327 (TDD)

Community Services for the Deaf
90 North Prospect Street
Akron, OH 44304
(216) 762-7601

Community Services for Deaf and
Hard-of-Hearing
Cincinnati Speech & Hearing Center
3006 Vernon Place
Cincinnati, OH 45219
(216) 221-0527 (Voice)
(216) 376-9351 (TDD)

Family Service Association
Community Service for the Deaf
184 Salem Avenue
Dayton, OH 45406
(513) 222-9481 (Voice)
(513) 222-7921 (TDD)

Rehabilitation Service of
North Central Ohio
Community Services for the Deaf
270 Sterkel Boulevard
Mansfield, OH 44907
(419) 756-1133

Youngstown Hearing & Speech Center
6505 Market Street
Youngstown, OH 44511
(216) 726-8855

Oklahoma

Tulsa Speech & Hearing Association
3815 South Harvard
Tulsa, OK 74135
(918) 747-2711

Pennsylvania

Berks County Association for the
  Hearing Impaired, Inc.
243 South 5th Street
Reading, PA 19602
(215) 374-7300 (Voice or TDD)

Interpreter Referral Service
4017 Ludlow Street
Philadelphia, PA 19104
(215) 222-0277

Pittsburgh Hearing, Speech & Deaf
  Services
1344 Fifth Avenue
Pittsburgh, PA 15219
(412) 281-1375 (Voice or TDD)

Rhode Island

Sargent Rehabilitation Center for Disorders
229 Waterman Street
Providence, RI 02906
(401) 751-3113

South Carolina

Hearing, Speech & Learning Center
811 Pendleton Street
9-11 Medical Court
Greenville, SC 29601
(803) 235-6065

Piedmont Speech & Hearing Center
397 Serpentine Drive
Spartanburg, SC 29303
(803) 582-2900

South Carolina Registry
  of Interpreters for the Deaf
572 Cecil Court
Spartanburg, SC 29301
(803) 583-4828
(803) 576-3155

South Dakota

South Dakota Association of the Deaf
Communication Service
114 South Main
Sioux Falls, SD 57102
(605) 339-6718

South Dakota Rehabilitation Services
State Office Building
Illinois Street
Pierre, SD 57501
(605) 224-3195

Tennessee

Chattanooga Regional Services
  for the Deaf
323 High Street
Chattanooga, TN 37403
(615) 265-4451 (Voice or TDD)

Interpreting Services for the Deaf
3548 Walker Avenue
Memphis, TN 38111
(901) 327-4233 (Voice or TDD)

Knoxville Area Communication Center
  for the Deaf, Inc.
139 Woodlawn Pike S.E.
Knoxville, TN 37920
(615) 577-4419 (Voice)
(615) 577-3559 (TDD)

League for the Hearing Impaired
Interpreter Referral Service
1810 Edge Hill Avenue
Nashville, TN 37212
(615) 320-7347 (Voice or TDD)
(615) 329-9271 (Voice or TDD)

Texas

Central Texas Council for the Deaf, Inc.
1012 North 22nd Street
Waco, TX 76707
(817) 753-8009 (Voice or TDD)

Corpus Christi Area Council for the Deaf
P.O. Drawer 9727
Corpus Christi, TX 78408
(512) 855-0581

Dallas Council for the Deaf
3115 Crestview
Dallas, TX 75235
(214) 521-0407

El Paso Council for the Hearing Impaired
1005 East Yandell Street
El Paso, TX 79924
(915) 566-2949

Gulf Coast Council for the Hearing
  Impaired
P.O. Box 13668
Houston, TX 77019
(713) 527-0222 (Voice)
(713) 527-0401 (TDD)

Lubbock County Services for the Deaf
P.O. Box 2321
Lubbock, TX 79407
(806) 744-2166

Panhandle Council for the Deaf
P.O. Box 30600
Amarillo, TX 79120
(806) 374-7171 (Voice or TDD)

Permian Basin Council for the
  Hearing Impaired
P.O. Box 7012
Midland, TX 79703
(915) 683-4651 (Voice)
(915) 697-3749 (TDD)

San Antonio Council for the Advancement of Services to the Deaf, Inc.
319 East Mulberry Road
San Antonio, TX 78212
(512) 734-9815 (Voice or TDD)

Silent Friends of Wichita Falls, Texas, Inc.
1005 ½ Baylor
P.O. Box 3243
Wichita Falls, TX 76309
(806) 723-2677 (Voice or TDD)

Southeast Texas Council for the
  Hearing Impaired
P.O. Box 10472, Lamar Station
Beaumont, TX 77710
(713) 838-8225 (Voice or TDD)

Tarrant County Services for the
  Hearing Impaired
2500 Lipscomb
Fort Worth, TX 76110
(817) 926-5305 (Voice or TDD)

Texarkana Area Services for the
  Hearing Impaired
222 West 5th Street
Texarkana, TX 75501
(214) 793-1841 (Voice or TDD)

Texoma Council for the Deaf
800 North Travis
Sherman, TX 75090
(214) 892-6531

Travis County Council for the Deaf
2201 Post Road, Room 100
Austin, TX 78704
(512) 444-3323 (Voice)
(512) 444-4181 (TDD)

Valley Association for the Hearing
  Impaired
Route 2, Box 247
Mercedes, TX 78570
(512) 565-5255 (Voice or TDD)

West Texas Service for the Deaf
1216 Mimosa
Abilene, TX 79603
(915) 692-4353 (Voice or TDD)

Virginia

Richmond Center for the Deaf
108 East Grace, P.O. Box 12084
Richmond, VA 23241
(804) 786-8432

Virginia Council for the Deaf
2407 West Main Street
Richmond, VA 23220
(804) 257-0986

Washington

Community Service Center for the Deaf
914 East Jefferson, Room 214
Seattle, WA 98122
(206) 322-4990 (Voice or TDD)

Appendix C

TUTORING AND NOTETAKING RESOURCES

California State University at
  Northridge
National Center on Deafness
Support Services to Deaf Students
18111 Nordhoff Street
Northridge, CA 91330
(213) 885-2614 (Voice or TDD)

Community College of Denver
Center for the Physically Disadvantaged
3645 West 11th Avenue
Westminster, CO 80030
(303) 466-8811 ext. 250
(Voice or TDD)

Johnson County Community College
Hearing-Impaired Program - Special
  Services Division
College Boulevard at Quivira Road
Overland Park, KS 66210
(913) 677-8572 (Voice or TDD)

Madonna College
Educational Support Services
36600 Schoolcraft
Livonia, MI 48150
(313) 591-5130 (Voice)
(313) 591-1203 (TDD)

National Technical Institute for the Deaf
  at Rochester Institute of Technology
Tutor/Notetaker Training Program
One Lomb Memorial Drive
P.O. Box 9887
Rochester, NY 14623
(716) 475-6493 (Voice or TDD)

Pasadena City College
Hearing-Impaired Program
1570 East Colorado Boulevard
Pasadena, CA 91106
(213) 578-7488 (Voice or TDD)

St. Paul Technical Vocational Institute
Program for Deaf Students
235 Marshall Avenue
St. Paul, MN 55102
(612) 221-1337 (Voice or TDD)

Seattle Central Community College
Regional Education Program for Deaf
  Students
1901 Broadway - 2NP304
Seattle, WA 98122
(206) 587-4138 (Voice or TDD)

Texas State Technical Institute
Deaf Student Services
Waco, TX 76705
(817) 799-3149 (Voice or TDD)

Utah State University
Facilitative Program for the Hearing
  Impaired
UMC 65
Logan, UT 84322
(801) 752-1923 (Voice)
(801) 753-3292 (TDD)

Waubonsee Community College
Hearing-Impaired Program
Route 47 at Harter Road
Sugar Grove, IL 60554
(312) 466-4811 ext. 215 (Voice)
(312) 466-4811 ext. 329 (TDD)

Appendix **D**

MEDIA RESOURCES

Adapted Media from Public Libraries

Gallaudet Media Distribution
Gallaudet College Library
7th Street and Florida Avenue
Washington, D.C. 20002

Handicapped Learner Materials
    Distribution Center
Indiana University
Audio-Visual Center
Bloomington, IN 47405

"Mediography on Deafness and the
    Deaf"
Document ED169 721 available
through Educational Resources
Information Center
Washington, D.C. 20202

Modern Talking Picture Service, Inc.
Captioned Films for the Deaf
5000 Park Street North
St. Petersburg, FL 33709

National Technical Institute for the
    Deaf at Rochester Institute of
    Technology
Division of Public Affairs
One Lomb Memorial Drive
P.O. Box 9887
Rochester, NY 14623

Media Not Already Adapted

National Information Center for
    Educational Media
University of Southern California
University Park
Los Angeles, CA 90007

Catalogs from media producers and
distributors, especially those
specializing in training materials.

Captioning of Media

The Caption Center*
WGBH-TV
125 Western Avenue
Boston, MA 02134
(617) 492-2777

Captioning Consultants*
40 Royal Oak Drive
Rochester, NY 14624
(716) 247-6756 (answering device)

National Captioning Institute, Inc.*
5203 Leesburg Pike
Falls Church, VA 22041
(703) 998-2430

National Technical Institute for the Deaf
    at Rochester Institute of Technology
Instructional Television Department
One Lomb Memorial Drive
P.O. Box 9887
Rochester, NY 14623
(716) 475-6374

PCI Recording Services*
Captioning Department
703 Atlantic Avenue
Rochester, NY 14609
(716) 288-5620

Rochester Upstate Productions
277 Alexander Street
Suite 510
Rochester, NY 14607
(716) 546-5417

* These agencies can caption materials
for you.

Appendix E

EQUIPMENT RESOURCES

Audio Graphic Supply
15207 Marquardt Avenue
Santa Fe Springs, CA 90670
(213) 921-0707

F.C. Sound**
43 Comanchee Circle
Rochester, NY 14624
(716) 235-5533

National Audiovisual Association*
3150 Spring Street
Fairfax, VA 22031
(703) 273-7200

National Technical Institute for the Deaf**
    at Rochester Institute of Technology
Training and Media Services Department
One Lomb Memorial Drive
P.O. Box 9887
Rochester, NY 14623
(716) 475-6425 (Voice or TDD)

R.F. Huether Industries**
494 Campbell Street
Rochester, NY 14609
(716) 235-5087

* Source offers product directories.

** Source can supply specific information
about inductive loop systems.

Appendix F

TDD INFORMATION RESOURCES

Hi-Line Communication Relay Service
Monroe County Association of Hearing
    Impaired
973 East Avenue
Rochester, NY 14604
(716) 244-1690

National Association of the Deaf
814 Thayer Avenue
Silver Spring, MD 20910
(almost every state has an
affiliate organization)

National Technical Institute for the Deaf
    at Rochester Institute of Technology
Training and Media Services Department
One Lomb Memorial Drive
P.O. Box 9887
Rochester, NY 14623
(716) 475-6425 (Voice or TDD)

Telecommunications for the Deaf, Inc.
814 Thayer Avenue
Silver Spring, MD 20910
(301) 587-1788

Appendix **G**

INTERNATIONAL RESOURCES

The following member organizations of the World Federation of the Deaf can be helpful in locating specific resources for hearing-impaired persons.

The Australian Federation of
 Adult Deaf Societies
101 Wellington Parade South
Melbourne East 3002
Victoria, Australia

Federation Nationale des Sourds
Avenue George - Henry 278
Woluwe Saint - Lambert
Brussels, Belgium

The Canadian Association of
 the Deaf
c/o E. Mo. Peske
248 Carleton Avenue
Ottawa, Ontario
Canada KIY 054

Danske Doves Landsforbund
Bryggervangen 19, 1
DK-2100 Copenhagen 0, Denmark

Confederation Nationale
 des Sourds de France
20 Rue de la Roquette
75011, Paris, France

The British Deaf Association
38 Victoria Place
Carlisle, CAI IHU Great Britain

Ente Nazionale Sordomuti
Via Gregorio VII, 120
00165, Rome, Italy

Japanese Federation of the Deaf
SK-Buil 130
Yanabuki-cho
Shinjuku-ku 162
Tokyo, Japan

Stichting Nederlandse
 Dovenraad
Postbus 19
3500 AA
Utrecht, Netherlands

The New Zealand Association
 of the Deaf
Box 408
Auckland 1, New Zealand

Federacion Nationales
 de Sociedades
de Sordomudos de Espana
Fuencarral 58, 2
Madrid 4, Spain

Deutscher Gehorlosen-Bund E.V.
Rothschildallee 16/A
6000 Frankfurt/Main 60 D.F.R.

ACKNOWLEDGMENTS

The following people contributed to the production of this manual:

NTID Project Development Team:

Robert Bowen, Media Production
Thomas Castle, Media Production
Cathy Chou, Media Production
Marcia Dugan, Public Affairs
Robert Iannazzi, Media Production
Sarah Perkins, Media Production
Laura Rogers, Administrative Services
Kathleen Sullivan, Public Affairs
Dean Woolever, Media Production
Willard Yates, Media Production

Content experts:

Dominic Bozzelli, Science and Engineering Support
Dr. Frank Caccamise, Communication Research
Dr. Diane Castle, Communication Instruction III
Dr. Kathleen Crandall, Communication Administration
Dr. Richard Curwin, Teaching Effectiveness
Elizabeth Ewell, Training and Media Services
Jaclyn Gauger, Communication Assessment and Advising
Katharine Gillies, Interpreting Services
Charles Johnstone, Training and Media Services
Dr. Gary Long, Educational Research and Development
Kevin Mogg, Interpreting Services
Stephen Nelson, Interpreting Services
Marie Raman, Science and Engineering Careers
Michael Rizzolo, Interpreting Services
Harriette Royer, director, Mental Health Chapter of the Health
    Association, Rochester, N.Y.
Linda Siple, Support Services Education
Dr. Joanne Subtelny, Communication Administration
Ruth Verlinde, Instructional Television
Jimmie Wilson, Tutor/Notetaker Training

Industrial Task Force:

Paul Ashton, 3M Corporation
Michael Dodis, General Motors Corporation
Richard Holan, U.S. Steel Corporation
Robin Hutchins, AT&T Company
George Kononenko, Hewlett-Packard Company
Gerald Lee, General Motors Corporation
Gary Snyder, IBM Corporation
Wilson Wong, IBM Corporation

"Accountants are familiar with the concept of profit and loss. What makes me different from other accountants is that I have been able to turn my losses into profits for me and my employer."

INDEX